WITHDRAWN

A FAR COUNTRY

A Far Country

A new play by

Henry Denker

Random House, New York

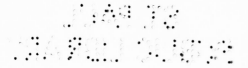

A FAR COUNTRY *was first presented by Roger L. Stevens and Joel Schenker at The Music Box, New York City, on April 4, 1961, with the following cast:*

(IN ORDER OF APPEARANCE)

SIGMUND FREUD (older)	Steven Hill
MARTHA BERNAYS FREUD (older), wife of Sigmund Freud	Salome Jens
THE NAZI	Wayne Carson
GORDON DOUGLAS, attaché, United States Consulate, Vienna	James Noble
MARTHA BERNAYS FREUD (at age twenty-seven)	Salome Jens
KATHY, the Freuds' maid of all work	Eda Reiss Merin
FREDERICK WOHLMUTH, Elizabeth's brother-in-law	Patrick O'Neal
SIGMUND FREUD (at age thirty-seven)	Steven Hill
AMALIE FREUD, Dr. Freud's mother	Lili Darvas
DOLFI FREUD, Dr. Freud's younger sister	Ellen Weston
ELIZABETH VON RITTER, a patient	Kim Stanley
DR. JOSEPH BREUER, an eminent doctor in Vienna	Sam Wanamaker

Directed by ALFRED RYDER
Associate Producer, LYN AUSTIN
Setting and Lighting by DONALD OENSLAGER
Costumes by ANN ROTH

THE SETTING

The office and anteroom of Sigmund Freud's modest flat in Vienna

This play is based on actual
events, authentically treated.
However, no real person portrayed
herein is still alive.

The soul of man is a far country which cannot be approached or explored.
—Heraclitus

ACT ONE

VIENNA, 1938. FREUD *is sitting in his wheel chair center, searching among his files.* MARTHA *is seated beside him. The doorbell rings, and a* NAZI *opens the door and steps in at attention to allow* DOUGLAS *to enter.*

FREUD (*To the* NAZI) They finally taught you to ring the bell, did they? That's no small achievement. With a bell and a dog Pavlov became a great man. So there's hope for you yet.
(*The* NAZI *steps out, closing the door*)

DOUGLAS Herr Doctor.

FREUD Herr Douglas! Is the car here?

DOUGLAS Not yet, Herr Doctor.

FREUD They changed their minds. They won't let us go.

DOUGLAS The plans remain exactly the same. You leave on the evening train. (*To* MARTHA) Madame.

MARTHA Herr Douglas.

FREUD One thing your embassy didn't explain to me. How is ransom paid in the twentieth century?

DOUGLAS It was a matter of bookkeeping, actually.

3

FREUD   Savages keep books too, do they?

DOUGLAS   All the assets which Madame Bonaparte had here in Austria, they were simply transferred.

FREUD   To the Nazis, hmm. Would you mind telling me how much? Or is it a State secret?

DOUGLAS   A quarter of a million schillings.

FREUD   Quarter of a million . . . did you hear that, Princess? A quarter of a million schillings.

DOUGLAS   Without Madame Bonaparte's help your departure could never have been arranged.

FREUD   I won't live long enough to repay her. You know that, don't you?

DOUGLAS   In England you'll have the best medical care.

FREUD   Including a cure for cancer?
   (*As he takes papers out of a portfolio*)

MARTHA   Sigmund!

FREUD   (*Holding up a special file*)   Found it! The case of Elizabeth von R.
   (*Opens the file. Holds out a dance program*)
   Still here. Look! A dance program is part of a medical case!
   Remember, Princess, we went to the Kuntzler Ball so I

4

could observe her? That was the night you said, "Sigmund, give up doctoring and become a dancing master. That way we can starve to music."

MARTHA   I never said that.

FREUD   (*To* DOUGLAS)   She can be very stubborn.

DOUGLAS   (*Handing the items to* FREUD)   Sir, your exit visas . . . railroad tickets. And my embassy instructed me to hand this to you personally.

(DOUGLAS *holds a letter-size envelope up to* FREUD *and offers it to him*)

FREUD   What is it? *You* read it.

DOUGLAS   (*Opens the letter, reads*)   "The Honorable Doctor Sigmund Freud. Nineteen Bergasse, Vienna. My dear Doctor, It is a matter of enormous relief that your freedom has finally been arranged. Half a century ago you unlocked the door to the human mind. Because of you every human being could at last look upon every other human being with more insight, more understanding, more compassion. Yet now you must be protected from hatred, ransomed from your native land. I know you have chosen England for your new home. But may I again extend to you the hospitality and protection of my country should you find it desirable to make yet another change. This nation and I stand ready to fulfill any demand you may make upon us. Faithfully yours, Franklin D. Roosevelt." (FREUD, *touched, holds out his hand.* DOUGLAS *gives him the letter*)   I'll be

5

back with the car at six-thirty. A man from the embassy will see to all this.

(*He indicates the remaining furnishings*)

MARTHA Thank you.

(DOUGLAS *exits*)

FREUD Forty-two years I practiced in this room . . . treated her in this room. And now "a man from the Embassy will see to all this." (*As he looks around the room*) June, and the windows are closed! Open them, Princess. (*She moves to open the windows*) Open them wide! (*She opens them wide*) Vienna on a summer day . . . the smell of it . . . the sounds of it. To leave Vienna for a new life, a new country, that takes courage.

MARTHA (*Before he can have regrets*) One last cup of Viennese coffee, Sigmund?

FREUD One last cup . . . (MARTHA *exits. He starts looking into the file again, reading*) "The patient Elizabeth von R." (*He interrupts himself suddenly with—*) English coffee? ? ? (*He spins his chair around*) Princess, do you realize that from now on there will be only English coffee. Now, that *does* take courage!

(*He wheels himself off during the above. The lights come down. The music of a waltz of the 1880's is heard. When the lights come up we are in the same apartment in 1893. Young* MARTHA FREUD *enters the office from the apartment, carrying a single rose in a vase and a box of cigars to the desk humidor*)

6

MARTHA (*Calling*) Kathy!

KATHY (*Enters from the apartment*) Yes, Madame.

MARTHA The fire.
(KATHY *crosses to fireplace in the corner, stage left*)

KATHY Yes, Madame.
(MARTHA *crosses to the anteroom table with the flower. She sets it down, and exits to the apartment. The doorbell rings*)

MARTHA (*offstage*) One moment, I'm coming!

KATHY (*Crosses eagerly to the front door*) I can answer the door, Madame!

MARTHA (*Offstage*) I'll answer it.

KATHY But I'm already at the door. What shall I do?

MARTHA (*Offstage*) All right, then, answer it.

KATHY Yes, Madame. (*Expectantly throwing open the door*) Herr Doctor, it's a pleasure to have you back . . . You, sir!

FREDERICK So, the Doctor is expected back today. Good! This time I will wait.
(*He enters.* KATHY *closes the front door*)

MARTHA (*Off*) Sigmund??

KATHY It's not Herr Doctor, Madame! It's that gentleman again. (FREDERICK *approaches the open office door, is curious about it, and enters.* KATHY *follows* FREDERICK)
Patients wait out there!

FREDERICK Surely the Doctor has nothing to hide. (KATHY *can find no answer, so he looks around the room, cautiously prodding*) How is it possible for a doctor with a large practice to spend so much time away from the city? Unless, of course, his practice is not so extensive.

KATHY Some of the most successful doctors in Vienna have their most extensive following in the obituary columns of the Vienna newspapers, sir! Extensive! Now, sir, you will have to wait out there. (FREDERICK *ignores her, being taken by the Faraday machine, which he inspects*) The Doctor doesn't allow anyone to touch that! (*He is not deterred. So she turns and starts toward the anteroom, calling out*) Madame! Madame!
     (KATHY *crosses and enters the apartment. Now the upstairs door opens quietly and* DR. SIGMUND FREUD, *a tense, defeated man enters, carrying a doctor's bag and small valise. He sets them down and drops his coat and hat on a chair. He takes up his doctor's bag and starts toward the office door when the apartment door opens and* MARTHA *enters*)

MARTHA Sigmund! (*They embrace, seeking comfort and warmth in each other. But her first touch of him warns her. She leans back, but* KATHY *enters. To be rid of her,* MARTHA *says—*) Kathy, the Doctor's coat and valise. And put on some water for coffee.

8

KATHY Yes, Madame. Welcome back, Herr Doctor.
(*She exits*)

MARTHA (*As soon as they're alone*) Sigmund? (*Feels his hand*) Ice cold . . . from the moment you boarded the train. And your migraine?

FREUD What does Joseph say about you?

MARTHA I am well. Exactly as I should be at three months. (*He kisses her but she interrupts when she remembers, and closes the door*) There's a patient in there. (*He reacts curiously*) He's come here every day for the last week. Today he insisted on waiting.

FREUD In there?

MARTHA He's a very persistent man.

FREUD If he's ill he has a right to be persistent. I'd better see him immediately.

MARTHA I could send him away.

FREUD No, I'll see him.
(*He turns to the door*)

MARTHA (*Finally she must say it*) Sigmund, are you sure you're able? (*He turns back to her*) Two nights on the train and you didn't sleep at all. I can tell. *And* your migraine too.

9

FREUD (*He nods, but when she moves to him*—) Princess, the patient is waiting. (*She gives way, exits to the apartment.* FREUD *sets himself to see the patient, enters the office carrying the doctor's bag, and closes the door*) And now, sir? (FREDERICK *rises, crosses, and very properly hands* FREUD *his card.* FREUD *glances at it*) "Frederick Wohlmuth" . . . Herr Wohlmuth, you're extremely anxious to see me, I hear.

FREDERICK If my actions seem a little unusual, it's the result of my experiences. I don't trust doctors!

FREUD (*Half resentful, half amused*) Oh?

FREDERICK In Vienna . . . No, let's be more accurate. In all Europe, the best doctors are not much better than the worst.

FREUD You've been coming here for a whole week just to tell me that?

FREDERICK I've come here because of what I'd heard about you. From another doctor.

FREUD (*Pointedly*) One of the best or one of the worst? (*He starts for his desk to set down the bag and to get a cigar*)

FREDERICK Taussig recommended you.

FREUD Taussig? He *is* one of the best.

FREDERICK He spoke very well of you. (*Seeking to elicit information*) Most especially how you cured a man of persistent headaches.

FREUD Taussig used the word "cured"?

FREDERICK Then there was such a case!

FREUD There was.

FREDERICK I had to make sure of that! Now we can talk. Dr. Freud, I . . .

FREUD (*Interrupting*) Mind you, I wouldn't use the word "cure" myself. The man's headaches may return. Is that your ailment? Headaches?

FREDERICK *My* ailment?

FREUD . . . Yes?

FREDERICK No. My sister-in-law is the patient.

FREUD And what are you? Her "ambassador"?

FREDERICK Allow me to explain. (*He sits in the chair* FREUD *indicates*) My sister-in-law's case is rather complicated . . . Actually I mean she's a rather special kind of patient. So, if you answer a few questions, I'll know if you can help her.

FREUD (*Interrupting*) Perhaps *you'd* better answer a few

questions first! That man with the headaches . . . do you know *how* I treated him?

FREDERICK With hypnosis. Correct?

FREUD Doesn't that frighten you? There are doctors in Vienna who would rather let a patient die than expose him to hypnosis.

FREDERICK Taussig warned me.

FREUD Did he also warn you that not everyone is susceptible to it?

FREDERICK Yes. But if she is, you can cure her of her pains. Which is more than any other doctor has been able to do!

FREUD First, Herr Wohlmuth, her pains . . . what kind . . . how long?
(*He begins lifting his instrument case, then takes a head of the god Janus out of his doctor's bag*)

FREDERICK As far as we can remember, they began almost six years ago.

FREUD That long?

FREDERICK Yes, they began shortly after the death of her father. She had exhausted herself nursing him.

FREUD I see.

FREDERICK Which may explain why I am so concerned about a sister-in-law. Who else is there to worry about her? Her mother is ill. Her sister, my own wife, dead almost three years.

FREUD So this responsibility has been thrust on you.

FREDERICK Not that I would avoid it—she's a very fine person; and—well, I will be completely honest about it, Doctor, I feel responsible for this.

FREUD Oh?

FREDERICK Yes. knowing how exhausted she was I never should have allowed her to take care of Charlotte. My wife. Yes, the unselfish way she nursed Charlotte in her last illness completely debilitated her, leaving her prey to the rheumatism. So it is my fault.

FREUD Rheumatism. That's the diagnosis?

FREDERICK Was. At the start. It's grown much worse. Despite all we've done. You know how it is, one doctor recommends another so you go from doctor to doctor . . .

FREUD (*Picking it up*) And from disillusionment to disillusionment.

FREDERICK Yes. But the man with the headaches, you cured him!

FREUD Herr Wohlmuth, where do her pains occur?

FREDERICK The legs. But what difference? Pain is pain, isn't it? If you helped that man . . .

FREUD (*Interrupting*) Simple headaches that yield to hypnotic suggestion are far different from six years of so-called rheumatic leg pains.

FREDERICK You could help her if you would only try!

FREUD (*Sharply silencing him*) Sir, don't saddle me with your enthusiasm. *Or* your ignorance!

FREDERICK You mean you won't . . . you can't condemn a girl to such suffering without even seeing her!

FREUD If I had a remedy and withheld it, I'd be condemning her.

FREDERICK But Taussig said . . .

FREUD Taussig said! Do you think I have some secret, some miracle that I'm hiding?
 (*Pushing the Faraday table forward*)
This is what we have! (*He urges* FREDERICK) Take off your glove. (*Frederick is obviously reluctant*) It won't hurt. (FREDERICK *takes off his glove.* FREUD *puts the machine in operation, runs a glass rod up and down, causing sparks to leap between the rod and the hand*) There. Hurt?

FREDERICK (*Finally at ease with it*) No.

FREUD Though it could be extremely painful if I increased the strength of the current.

FREDERICK Creates a sort of tingling sensation.

FREUD Seems to make the blood course through the veins, doesn't it?

FREDERICK Actually pleasant, in a way. Elizabeth won't mind this at all, I can assure you!

FREUD There's just one thing wrong with it.

FREDERICK What?

FREUD It doesn't work! Totally and completely useless.
(He pushes the table back into position)

FREDERICK In that case . . . what's it doing here?

FREUD This is the latest "scientific discovery." Yes, that's what we nerve specialists call it. And we use it at the slightest provocation. We use it for cases of paralysis with no physical basis. We use it for pain with no discernible cause. We use it and use it and use it! But not one of us has ever seen it cure anything! Perhaps I exaggerate. Actually it does divert the patient from his pain, gives him a momentary sense of well-being. But it cures nothing. Now, I'm sorry. I'm extremely tired. One doesn't get much sleep on trains.

FREDERICK Evidently.
(The doorbell rings)

FREUD You are dealing with ignorant men and have been

ever since your sister-in-law became ill. From what you've described, there's nothing I can do for her.

FREDERICK If you saw her . . .

FREUD No!
  (MARTHA *enters and goes to the door*)

FREDERICK But she's in the vicinity . . .
  (AMALIE *enters, followed by* DOLFI)

FREUD It would do no good.

FREDERICK I could bring her here immediately!

FREUD (*Interrupting with finality*) No! (*His intensity having silenced* FREDERICK, *he softens*) This is the kindest way. In the long run. Good day, Herr Wohlmuth!
  (FREDERICK *relents, turns. He opens the office door and closes it behind him. He faces the women, then exits*)

MARTHA Mama . . . Dolfi!
  (AMALIE *holds aside the pastry box she is carrying, to allow* MARTHA *to give her a dutiful kiss*)

AMALIE Well, child, he is back . . .
  (*She watches* FREDERICK *exit*)

MARTHA Quarter of an hour ago.

AMALIE Good! And you, what does the doctor say?

16

MARTHA For a woman three months pregnant, everything is quite normal.

AMALIE Have you served his coffee?

MARTHA Not yet.

AMALIE (*Handing the pastry box to her*) Set these on the tray. Linzer torte!
(*She takes off her gloves and cape*)

MARTHA (*As she takes the box and sees*) From Dehmel's! Mama . . . so expensive!

AMALIE (*Giving her cape to* MARTHA) Permit me one little extravagance on the day my son returns. Now go, dear.

DOLFI I'll help!

AMALIE (*To prevent* DOLFI *from warning* MARTHA) It's only a few slices. She doesn't need any help.
(*But they have already gone.* AMALIE *moves to the office door and opens it.* FREUD *is writing a note, but the opening of the door interrupts him. He sees* AMALIE)

FREUD Mama!
(*He puts aside his pen, and goes to kiss her hand. She takes his hands*)

AMALIE Welcome home, my son. So cold . . .

FREUD (*Indicating the window*) Yes—have you ever seen such a nasty March? It even feels like snow.

AMALIE   For me the colder the better. Or have you forgotten? Anyhow I feel warmer when you're here. But I'm interrupting, hmm?

FREUD   No. I'm only writing a note to Joseph to let him know I'm back.

AMALIE   Breuer?

FREUD   Yes.

AMALIE   Then write! After all, Breuer is an important doctor!

FREUD   (*Pleasantly reprimanding her for interfering*) Mama . . .

AMALIE   Your note! (*After a moment, and trying to make it seem casual*) Tell me, is Dr. Breuer influential at the Medical Academy?

FREUD   Mama, you know Dr. Breuer is influential everywhere. (DOLFI *opens the door and rushes into the office,* KATHY *is behind her, carrying a tray with coffee.* MARTHA *follows with the cake plate*)

DOLFI   Sigmund!

FREUD   (*He rises, comes to greet her*) Dolfi! You too? I should go away more often! (*He kisses her, then looks at her*) Ah, such a pretty blouse! And such tiny stitches. Mama, you are an artist, no question!

AMALIE (*Irked by undeserved praise*) Dolfi made it herself.

FREUD Naturally. It's an inherited talent. (*He spies the cake tray, can't resist snatching a taste and savoring it*) Whoever is guilty of *this* extravagance, thank you. (*He kisses* AMALIE. KATHY *crosses, gives* FREUD *the coffee. He takes it, at the same time handing her the note*) Kathy, take this . . . to Doctor Breuer!
(KATHY *exits*)

MARTHA Dolfi.

DOLFI Thank you.

AMALIE (*Settling down and trying to make her questions appear usual, pleasant*) Well, Sigmund . . . your journey to Nancy . . . your patient . . . how did it go?

FREUD Hopeless. Dr. Bernheim couldn't help her either.

AMALIE Oh? Too bad. But, at least, about *this* trip there won't be any report to the Medical Academy.

FREUD Mama, that's the second time!

AMALIE (*The complete innocent*) Second time . . . ?

FREUD The second time you've mentioned the Academy.

MARTHA (*Having been warned by* DOLFI) Sigmund, not now, not today. You're very tired and . . .

FREUD Mama!

AMALIE Months ago, after you came back from your studies in Paris, did you make a speech at the Academy?

FREUD Yes.

AMALIE How could you have done such a dangerous thing?

FREUD To confront old doctors with new ideas may be foolish, but not dangerous.

AMALIE I've been told that it is!

FREUD Who frightened you so? Mama?

AMALIE You've heard me mention an acquaintance, a Frau Schoenfeld? Her son was at the meeting when you gave that . . . that report.

FREUD I merely read a paper on "Hysteria in the Human Male." Based on my research under Dr. Charcot. That's what I was sent to Paris to do. So let's not make it sound like some illegal activity, hmm?

AMALIE They didn't agree with you!

FREUD No, they didn't.

AMALIE The doctors at that meeting were successful, established, reputable men?

FREUD But in this instance, completely wrong.

AMALIE Right or wrong, my son, where is a nerve specialist to expect patients, but from other doctors?

FREUD Aha! I see.

AMALIE So no more speeches, please!

FREUD Mama, disagreement is as much a part of the Academy as cigar smoke. So there's nothing to worry about.

AMALIE If you say so, my son. I will not worry. Why should I? Merely because some doctors insisted you *resign* from the Academy?
(MARTHA *reacts. She never knew till now.* FREUD *exchanges looks with her*)

FREUD In the heat of argument men say rash things.

AMALIE But they did say it!

FREUD They won't expel me!

AMALIE They will if one of your patients goes mad!

DOLFI Mama! You promised you wouldn't say anything like that!

AMALIE Dr. Schoenfeld said . . .

FREUD (*Outraged*) You discussed me with Dr. Schoenfeld?

AMALIE (*Too innocently*) Frau Schoenfeld and I were having tea. He came by. He raised the subject. What could I do? Dr. Schoenfeld said you use hypnosis in your practice! And it's very dangerous.

FREUD Schoenfeld is no authority!

AMALIE Perhaps not. But he is not being asked to resign! Sigmund . . . a Jew is born with enough enemies! Why must you antagonize everyone? You could earn as much as any good doctor in Vienna . . . (*Indicating* MARTHA) . . . if only she wanted it.

MARTHA Mama, please. Stay to dinner, and we'll talk later.

AMALIE Of course, protect him from me! You'll protect him into failure.

FREUD Mama! You will discuss none of this with Martha.

AMALIE There! There we have it. You're stubborn, she protects you. She's wrong, you defend her. And meantime your life, your career are being wasted! When you were born the midwife held you up. Look, she said, a sign. There was a caul covering your tiny wrinkled face. And I knew this child, this son of mine, is a special child of greatness, of genius.

FREUD (*To* MARTHA) Not yet an hour old and already I showed signs of genius.

AMALIE (*His joke only intensifies her feeling*) Has any

mother had more proof? First in your class every year. Prizes, scholarships! And when you began to study medicine, you proved it even more. Famous doctors complimenting you on your research, your brilliant diagnoses. You have no right to endanger the gifts you were born with.

FREUD (*Picking up a long-time phrase of hers, and finishing the sentence with her*) The gifts you were born with.

AMALIE (*Hurt, petulant*) Don't you dare make fun of me.

FREUD Mama, they've upset you with lies!

AMALIE Have they? (*As though playing a trump card*) It is impossible for hysteria to occur in the human male.

FREUD Oh, I see. Schoenfeld?

AMALIE Schoenfeld! He said it's a medical fact! The whole Academy agrees with him. He said the very word hysteria comes from the Greek . . . hysteron . . . it means . . . it . . . (*She is suddenly embarrassed*)

FREUD (*Smiling at her embarrassment*) It means . . . the womb!

AMALIE (*Now that he's said it, she can be firm*) Yes! So hysteria is a female word for a female condition. Every doctor knows that.

FREUD Every doctor and his mother, evidently.
(DOLFI *laughs*)

AMALIE At least Schoenfeld didn't treat me like an ignorant woman who wouldn't understand!

FREUD (*To soothe her, he goes to her, takes her hand, starts to explain*) Mama, when I was a student . . . I used to bring home specimens to work on—nerve specimens . . .

AMALIE (*With distaste*) You showed them to me! I remember.
(*She withdraws her hand*)

FREUD Always I was searching for nerve damage, brain damage. If a person during his lifetime had a paralyzed leg or a constant tremor of the hand you would discover during the autopsy what part of his brain or nervous system was damaged and caused the condition.

AMALIE You saw it . . . under your microscope?

FREUD Yes.

AMALIE Then how could there be any dispute?

FREUD Because there *are* cases where one can't see it.

AMALIE Not even you?

FREUD (*Indulging her pride*) Not even I.

AMALIE If you couldn't see it, it wasn't there!

FREUD Mama, your reasoning is not quite correct. But your

conclusion is. It wasn't there. And that's the ridiculous mystery of it. It's as if Newton's apple had fallen up. It is impossible. We know it. Yet it happens. A patient, male or female, looked like a paralytic, walked like one, all his life. But when you did the autopsy, no physical trace, no wound, no scar, nothing! Effect without cause!

AMALIE Sigmund, if an injury is not physical, what can it be?

FREUD It could be a wound in the mind, in the soul.

AMALIE That's what you told them at the Academy? Of course, they told you to resign! Sigmund, what are you, a doctor or a priest? What have you to do with souls? To heal sickness, to ease pain is the finest work a man can do. Do it. Practice medicine like all good Viennese doctors. They're the best in the world!

FREUD Why do you think I just took my patient all the way to Nancy? Why? Because there was no help for her here! I took her like a mother carries a dying child to a holy shrine. Not knowing, just hoping. We can't help her and Bernheim is having unusual results with hypnosis, so try hypnosis. I can't hypnotize her? Try Bernheim. So we go. And for seven days he tries to hypnotize her. But nothing happens! Nothing! And then there is no place to go but home, to Vienna, where we *know* there is no help. All the way back her pain is worse. And now I haven't even the anaesthetic of hope to hold out to her. The whole journey is a terrible, painful failure!

AMALIE But not your fault!

FREUD Not my fault! Still someone has to keep searching! So maybe one day there will be a spark of light, a flicker of understanding, an explanation of why unseen wounds can cripple, can destroy!

AMALIE Exactly like your Papa. Everyone said leave Freiburg, go into business in Vienna. But he knew better than anyone. Sigmund, you are no longer a child. You're a man with responsibilities to yourself, to your wife, soon to a baby.

MARTHA (*Interrupting*) Let me speak for his wife, if you don't mind!

AMALIE Then speak! You owe him that much! He sacrificed enough for you!

FREUD Mama! You will leave the Academy to the doctors! And my wife to me! And you will have to believe that I am not twelve years old! That I know the possible from the impossible. A man was here a little while ago, asking me to see a new patient. With all the same familiar symptoms. And I sent him away! But not to please the other doctors! Or the Academy! I sent him away because there's nothing I can do for the patient!

AMALIE You still blame yourself . . .

FREUD I blame myself—I blame all of us! Charlatans! That's what we are. "Frau Scholz, your headaches grow worse? Take hot baths twice a day. Oh, you have? Well, then take cold ones. Oh, I see. Well, then in such a case we always prescribe dark glasses. Blue? Oh, no! In a case like yours,

26

red! Always red. Of course we're sure! We don't reach these conclusions lightly. We are scientific . . . accurate." We are frauds! We know nothing.

AMALIE   Sigmund.

FREUD   (*Exploding*)   I won't hear any more!
  (AMALIE *is hurt and hushed*)

MARTHA   Mama, please, he's very tired . . .

AMALIE   No, child, don't comfort me. Don't even try.
  (*She goes into the anteroom to get her things and moves to the front door.* DOLFI *follows*)

FREUD   (*He follows to apologize*)   Mama, wait!

AMALIE   You talk about unseen wounds . . . I could tell you about some.
  (*She exits*)

FREUD   Mama! (DOLFI *exits with* AMALIE. FREUD *turns back to the office to find* MARTHA *silent, staring*) I know. The threat at the Academy . . . I should have told you about that. I . . . forgot. (*She doesn't answer*) I didn't forget. I . . . I didn't want you to worry, especially now.

MARTHA   Why did you tell her you turned a patient away?

FREUD   I did turn a patient away. (*Her surprise makes him admit*) Yes . . . the migraine too. Every time I board the train! Why? I reason with myself, I say to myself . . . the train speeds through the night, on time, safe, under the hand of a capable engineer. And if I have any doubt, the whistle sounds to remind me, the engineer is alert, everything is as it should be. Yet to me it's not a train. It's a demon let loose, hurtling through the night, carrying me to my death! I doze off for a moment and the whistle screams, cutting into me like a knife. I'm awake again. And in pain. And I cry out, "Physician, heal thyself." How . . . with what . . . ignorance? I take a patient all the way to Nancy when it is *I* who really needs a cure! Maybe I went hoping Bernheim could do something for me! If only I could be free of the pain, the panic, I would be successful. Or maybe it's the other way round. If I were successful—like Joseph—then perhaps the headaches, the discomfort would disappear. I need success!

MARTHA Success.

FREUD Yes. Years ago, I wrote you from Paris—"I am not a genius. I am not even very gifted. I have a large capacity for work and that's all."

MARTHA (*She goes to him*) "I have often felt that I have inherited all the defiance and all the passions with which our ancestors defended their temple, and I would gladly sacrifice my life for one great moment in history." You wrote me that, too.

FREUD (*Interrupting*) Then I had a future. The future is here! And what am I? A thirty-seven-year-old man who can't support his wife! And soon won't be able to support his child either! And, Princess . . . I'm *afraid*. (*She reacts*)

I am! Mama only talked about dismissal from the Academy. They could bar me from the hospital. Even question my right to practice. What would I become? A laboratory assistant who spends his life feeding guinea pigs and rabbits? Do you want that to happen to me, do you? I was an excellent diagnostician once, wasn't I? I will be again.

MARTHA Mama was right—

FREUD (*To avoid talking about it, he interrupts, relating to the Janus on the desk*) There is the real villain! I couldn't afford it and I couldn't resist it. So I bought it. Janus! God of Beginnings. Today is a beginning. From now on, a new, a prosperous Dr. Freud. And able to afford not only this, but originals! (*He admires the piece*) Janus, god with two faces. This fierce one . . . looking back on the lean years. This one, looking ahead to the fat years . . .

MARTHA (*Persisting*) Mama was right about one thing. It is my fault. The cocaine anaesthetic was your discovery.

FREUD Koller proved it first.

MARTHA And who first showed it to him? You! And you would have got the credit for it. *You* would be known as the man who made delicate eye surgery possible, not Koller. If you hadn't left your research to come visit me in Wandsbek!

FREUD Princess!

MARTHA With your name on that discovery they wouldn't dare attack you at the Academy. Or threaten you!

FREUD Have I ever blamed you for that? (*She admits he hasn't. He takes her by the arms*) Then don't blame yourself. That's ancient history. Forget she ever said it. Promise? Yes, I know. I shouldn't have left you. Not now. After all, when you woke and wanted fresh strawberries, who was there to roam the streets of Vienna in the dead of night searching for them?

MARTHA Not strawberries. Veal in sour cream!

FREUD But you don't even like veal in sour cream!

MARTHA I know.
(*They embrace, but are interrupted by the doorbell*)

FREUD Kathy will answer it.

MARTHA You sent her to Joseph's.

FREUD Of course! I won't leave you again. Ever!
(*The bell sounds again, more insistently now.* MARTHA *goes to answer it.* FREUD *turns back to the desk. Meantime,* MARTHA *opens the front door and* FREDERICK *enters briskly. She precedes him to the office door*)

MARTHA One moment please. (*To warn him*) Sigmund . . .
(*She picks up tray, and exits*)

FREUD (*Sees* FREDERICK) I thought I made myself clear.

FREDERICK (*Closes the office door*) She insisted. I couldn't refuse.

30

FREUD I told you I could do nothing.

FREDERICK If you just talk to her it might help in some way.

FREUD My dear man, I told you . . .
 (*The front door being open, we hear—*)

ELIZABETH (*Off*) . . . and then come back for us! Promptly,
Peter!

FREDERICK See her, just this once!

FREUD Sorry.
 (*He opens the door to find her entering*)

ELIZABETH Dr. Freud?

FREUD (*Confronted, he must answer*) Fräulein . . . I hear you
are determined to see me.

ELIZABETH Since I was near by, I thought I might as well.
Especially today. I love the feel of March—the wind. Don't
you? (*He goes to her, gestures her into the office and then
closes the front door and follows her in. She stops, admires
the room, then indicates a chair*) This one, Doctor?

FREUD Allow me . . .
 (*She reaches the chair, eases herself into it carefully, at
the same time releasing her crutches to* FREUD, *who
takes them and turns to put them against the wall till
she interrupts him*)

31

ELIZABETH I would like them *here,* please.

FREUD (*Intrigued by this, he gives the crutches back to her. Studies her a moment, then goes to take his place behind the desk. He asks provocatively*) Comfortable?

ELIZABETH I'm afraid the only one who's uncomfortable here is *you,* Doctor. You see, this is a game we play, Frederick and I. He insists that I see doctor after doctor after doctor, in the very forlorn hope that one of them will be able to cure me. And I go, only to indulge him, for he is rather sweet, when he is not being too insistent.

FREUD He's insistent. *I* can tell you that.

FREDERICK I have to be! Otherwise, she would never go . . .

ELIZABETH (*Interrupting*) I should also have told you, Doctor, the most painful thing one can do to Frederick is tell the truth about him in his presence.

FREDERICK Elizabeth . . .

ELIZABETH You see, even such a *small* truth makes him very uncomfortable. Was it my idea to come here?

FREDERICK Please, Elizabeth . . .

ELIZABETH And when I refused, he suggested he would see you first, would find out about this "Dr. Freud," and then meet me at the milliner's and describe you to me? And only *then* would I have to decide about coming here? Did I say that? Or did you?

FREDERICK Elizabeth! Really . . .

ELIZABETH It was only when he came back and said the doctor didn't *want* to see me, that I was intrigued. Yes, intrigued! No doctor's ever said *that* before. And didn't I say, as long as I was close by and it was convenient, I would see him? But it had to be today or not at all? Because we do this for *your* sake, not *mine!* We know nothing can come of it! Now I know you must go through a certain routine examination.

FREUD (*Provoked, he seeks to elicit a reaction*) We could dispense with the routine, if you resent it so.

ELIZABETH Oh, let us have it over with. After all, the carriage is gone. I asked Peter to come back for me as soon as he had circled the park twice.

FREUD Fast or slow? (ELIZABETH *reacts, herself taken aback now*) I only wanted to know if we have fifteen minutes or thirty?

ELIZABETH (*Laughing*) It usually only takes fifteen.

FREUD (*Rising, he makes the usual gesture to assist her*) Let me help you to the examining couch.

ELIZABETH I prefer to sit.

33

FREUD Lying down might be more comfortable.

ELIZABETH I prefer to sit!
(*The strangeness of her insistence makes* FREUD *relent.
He moves a hassock into place, swings her chair around
so that he can examine her. But when he bends and
reaches for her legs, she suddenly tenses. He does not
persist*)

FREDERICK Do you wish me to step outside?

FREUD It won't be necessary.

FREDERICK As you say, Herr Doctor.

FREUD Tell me, Fräulein . . .
(*He gropes for her name*)

ELIZABETH . . . von Ritter.

FREUD Fräulein von Ritter, this pain in your legs . . . when
did it start?

FREDERICK As I told you, Doctor, the first pain was about six
years ago when her father . . . (FREUD *interrupts by looking
sharply at* FREDERICK, *who acknowledges the rebuke*) Sorry.

FREUD Fräulein?

ELIZABETH In its serious form, about *two* years ago.

FREUD (*Indicating he would like to examine her legs*) May I?

34

ELIZABETH Should you be the only doctor in Vienna who hasn't?

(*This time she allows him to lift her legs to the hassock*)

FREUD As you said yourself, we must go through the routine. Exactly what do you feel? Can you describe it?

ELIZABETH (*As he presses and tests her reflexes*) It ... it seems to start here ... (*She indicates her thighs*) Then it moves down the legs ...

FREUD But is it always worse in the thighs?

ELIZABETH Much.

FREUD A constant kind of pain or stabbing?

ELIZABETH Constant, in the beginning, slight, though noticeable, of course.

FREUD Do you remember the first time you felt the severe pain?

ELIZABETH Yes. We were all in the country. Except my father, of course. He was dead by that time. But the rest of us were there, my mother, my sister Charlotte, Frederick, friends. Some of us had gone for a long walk ...

FREDERICK Tell the Doctor how first you spent the whole day taking care of Charlotte!

FREUD (*A rebuke to* FREDERICK) Please?

35

FREDERICK It's important, isn't it?

FREUD If you persist, I will have to ask you to leave!

FREDERICK Sorry.

FREUD (*Touches* ELIZABETH's *leg*) Now, Fräulein . . .

ELIZABETH There was a whole group of us . . .

FREUD Yes—
   (*He rises and starts toward the desk*)

ELIZABETH (*Suddenly tense*) Is something wrong?

FREUD (*Trying to be casual in face of her sudden tenseness*)
   Only some instruments for my examination. Now, you
   were telling us about that walk . . .
   (*He returns and sets the case on the floor*)

ELIZABETH There . . . there was a whole group of us and we
   walked to the top of the hill overlooking a little village, a
   summer resort. We sat there a long time, had a great excited discussion about something. You know how *young
   people* are.
   (*As he opens the case, she furtively tries to see what's
   in it. He catches her looking*)

FREUD (*Trying to be casual*) Lower your stocking, please.

ELIZABETH (*Pointedly*) Which one?

36

FREUD (*It's a curious question, but he says pleasantly—*) The right one, please.
> (*She stares at him a moment, then lowers her stocking. As she does this,* FREUD *takes a needle out of the case*)

ELIZABETH (*Suddenly*) What's that?

FREUD Only a needle. Routine in this kind of examination. You must know that. Now, what about *young people* and their . . .(*He pricks her several times with no reaction*) . . . and their discussions?

ELIZABETH (*Concerned with what he is doing*) I don't remember any more. Besides, what difference does it make? Is it important?

FREUD Do young people ever have *un*important discussions? *Do* they, Fräulein?

ELIZABETH (*Suddenly*) You've found out something! Tell me!

FREUD (*Just enough to draw her out*) Found out?

ELIZABETH Yes!

FREUD What makes you think I could discover anything of consequence in so short and so "routine" an examination?

ELIZABETH When you've been to as many doctors as I have, you can tell! You think that there'll be a complete paralysis. And I'll have to spend the rest of my life in a wheel chair!

FREUD Fräulein, have there been pains that you've never mentioned to anyone?

ELIZABETH No.

FREUD Yet you have a definite feeling that it will get worse. Why?

ELIZABETH It always has. What can the next step be but a wheel chair?

FREUD (*Challengingly*) Would you find it easier to use one *now?*

ELIZABETH No. I'll walk as long as I'm able. Even if it has to be on these.
(*She indicates her crutches*)

FREUD Yes, I would keep walking, if I were you. Though walking is very painful, isn't it? Not as painful as sitting, as you are now. Yet lying down is somehow worst of all. Why?

ELIZABETH I didn't say that, did I?

FREUD No. You didn't. (*Seeking a new line of attack*) There seems to have been an unusual amount of sickness in your family.

38

ELIZABETH Did Frederick also tell you that every other doctor says my affliction is not hereditary?

FREUD You resent his telling me anything about you. Why?

ELIZABETH What happened to my family is unfortunate. But it is *my* sorrow and I hope you will forgive me if I think that sorrow is a private matter.

FREUD (*Pointedly*) Or a way of life?

ELIZABETH (*Provoked, she nevertheless persists*) If one *is* afflicted, one should face it with dignity, accept reality, and not go thrusting oneself on every doctor with an open door.

FREUD How else is one to find a cure?

ELIZABETH People who do that do so more to find pity than a cure, I'm afraid! I want no one feeling sorry for me. Nor do I feel sorry for myself. Instead of brooding, I have made a life for myself. Full, rich, satisfying. *And* useful. I have my poetry . . . and some professors of our acquaintance at the University call my poems quite good.

FREDERICK They even insisted she submit them to the Quarterly!
    (ELIZABETH *laughs lightly, as though embarrassed*)

FREUD And did you?— Did you?

ELIZABETH (*Her laugh suddenly gone*) I have my poetry . . . my painting . . . my charity—I sew for the poor. With my own fingers. So you see, the future holds no threat of boredom for me, no terror. In fact, you might say I have only one problem. Frederick's unreasonable need to have me cured . . . when everyone knows it can never be! Well, that concludes the interview, I imagine! Frederick, see if Peter is back with the carriage!

(KATHY *and* BREUER *enter through the front door*)

FREUD Tell me, Fräulein, when did you first come to the conclusion that it was hopeless? (KATHY *knocks on the office door and opens it.* BREUER *is just behind her*) Kathy, I've told you never to interrupt when there is a patient in here!

KATHY I'm sorry, Herr Doctor, I didn't know!

BREUER It's my fault, Sigmund. Forgive me!

FREUD Joseph!

BREUER I will come back later.
(*He starts out*)

FREUD Wait, Joseph! (*To* ELIZABETH) Excuse me a moment, please?

ELIZABETH I am quite ready to leave. Thank you.

FREUD (*Very firmly*) One moment, please! (*She looks at him angrily. He stares her down. She finally is forced to settle back. Only then does* FREUD *go out to see* BREUER. *When*

FREDERICK *moves to comfort her she averts her head, sees the Janus on the desk*) Joseph!

BREUER Sorry to have interrupted you, Sigmund. But it's an emergency.

FREUD (*Sobered suddenly*) Oh?

BREUER A patient of mine, at the hospital. A bad postpartum reaction.

FREUD (*Relieved, he jokes*) Since her baby was born she refuses to see her husband. Can you blame her?

BREUER She won't eat. And when we force her, she cannot retain food.

FREUD I see. But what can I do?

BREUER Make her eat. By hypnotic suggestion.

FREUD And risk your reputation too?
(*He says it as a joke*)

BREUER I don't care about risk! Just make her eat, before she dies. I know you can do it. Now, can you come at once?

FREUD Joseph, you've done hypnosis in the past. Why do you need me?

BREUER (*Intensely*) Please, Sigmund!

FREUD Of course. Give me a moment . . . (*As he turns away, it occurs to him. He turns back to* BREUER) Joseph, take a look at this young woman. A perfect case of hysterical pain. Yet the strangest case I've ever seen.

BREUER Hysterics are all strange.

FREUD I apply pressure, her pain increases.

BREUER Naturally.

FREUD I stab her with the needle and her pain disappears. (BREUER *reacts*) Completely! Have a look at her. Then I'll go to the hospital with you.
(*To urge him,* FREUD *relieves him of his hat and the file he carries*)

BREUER That file's for you. (*Puzzled,* FREUD *looks at him*) You'll call it a bribe to make you go to the hospital with me. Perhaps. But that case history of mine, the one you keep asking about . . .

FREUD (*With anticipation now*) The one that convinced you of the value of hypnosis? So you've finally decided to let someone see it!

BREUER Not someone! You! Make sure no one else does see it.

FREUD Of course. Now, examine her. Notice in particular, the total lack of reaction on the sides of the calves.

Steven Hill, Sam Wanamaker, and Kim Stanley, as
SIGMUND FREUD, JOSEPH BREUER, and ELIZABETH VON RITTER

BREUER (*Taken aback*) Her affliction is in the legs?

FREUD Yes. What difference does that make?

BREUER Why . . . why none, none at all.
(*They enter the office*)

FREUD Fräulein von Ritter—Herr Wohlmuth . . . A distinguished colleague . . . Dr. Joseph Breuer.

BREUER Fräulein . . .

FREDERICK Dr. Breuer! Of course!

FREUD Fräulein von Ritter, we're extremely fortunate that Dr. Breuer happened to come by, so I asked him if he would examine you.

ELIZABETH I will not be put on display!

FREUD Display? This is a medical consultation!

ELIZABETH I will not be exhibited! I will not be examined by any more doctors! Frederick! Please take me home!
(*When he does not assist her, she starts to rise, gets her crutches in place*)

FREDERICK Elizabeth! Please! Please?
(*She is not deterred;* FREDERICK *tries to intercept her*)

FREUD No, no, let her go. Let her go! Other girls . . . as young, as attractive, would want to walk and run and dance! But not she! She has her painting, her poetry. Her fine and generous sewing for the poor. With "her own fingers," mind you! (ELIZABETH *stops, arrested. Then turns, continues toward the door*) Is that where you're going now, Fräulein? Is that why you have no time for us who would try to help you? Or are you really straining so desperately to reach the one thing for which you've been faithfully preparing yourself for two long years now . . . your wheel chair? ?

(*The word "wheel chair" makes her turn to face* FREUD. FREUD *challenges her with his stare. She wavers, then finally starts back toward the office*)

The Curtain Falls

ACT TWO

Scene 1

Time: afternoon, two weeks later.

At rise: we discover ELIZABETH *seated in an armchair, with her feet on the hassock.* FREUD *sits opposite her, using a shiny object on a chain like a metronome to focus her attention while he tries to hypnotize her. Her crutches are resting against the upstage wall.*

FREUD Concentrate . . . follow closely . . . let your eyes follow and be relaxed . . . Now think of sleep . . . tired and you want only to sleep . . . sleep . . . sleep . . . Now your arms are getting heavy . . . let them go. Your hands. Let them fall away. Good. Elbows—let them drop—your shoulders—let them go . . . Let them fall. Good. Now, Elizabeth—the sky is very dark—and you are floating . . . floating. (*Cautiously, since it would be the first time she is under*) Elizabeth . . . do you hear me? (*She nods like one in a hypnotic trance*) Raise your right hand . . . raise it. (*She obeys*) Now lower it. Good (*She does*) Hold it out . . . rigidly. Good. Lower it. (*She holds out her arm, straight and stiff.* FREUD, *to test, presses down on her arm but she resists*) Elizabeth . . . when I instruct you, you will move your legs. And when you do, this time, you will *not feel pain.* Understand? No pain! Now move your legs!

ELIZABETH (*Eyes still closed, she taunts him*) Well, I finally found out what you wanted me to do! (*She opens her eyes, but he does not join her joke*) You're angry with me.

47

FREUD Yes.

ELIZABETH I'm sorry. I try. Believe me, I do. Is there something terribly wrong with me?

FREUD (*To cover his own concern and reassure her*) Not everyone is susceptible.

ELIZABETH And if one isn't? Then there's nothing you can do for her, is there?

FREUD I've seen patients not responsive one day who were the next.

ELIZABETH (*Suddenly, and tense*) It's been the "next day" for twelve days now! And nothing has happened.

FREUD (*He presses her hand*) We must be patient. That will be all for today.
     (*He turns away to get her crutches but the moment of contact has an effect on* ELIZABETH. *To keep from being sent away she asks*)

ELIZABETH When I leave here, what do you do?

FREUD (*Turning back without her crutches*) Do?

ELIZABETH The rest of your time . . . your days . . . your nights? . . .

FREUD (*Lightly*) Oh. People always think that doctors lead such interesting lives. The truth is, we do the same as everyone else. Work, read, go to the theatre, argue about politics . . .

ELIZABETH Even with your wives?

FREUD (*More soberly*) Sometimes.
(*He starts to turn back but she arrests him with—*)

ELIZABETH Do you ever think about what *I* do when I leave here?

FREUD Write poetry . . . paint . . . sew for the poor, if I remember.
(*He begins to be aware of her desperate effort to stay on*)

ELIZABETH I have a confession to make . . . My poetry . . . it's not very good.

FREUD But you mentioned some professors at the University . . .

ELIZABETH They were being gentlemen more than scholars, I'm afraid. (*Changing the subject quite suddenly*) Sometimes, sitting out there waiting for you, I see her . . . She's a very devoted person. And she carries herself with a kind of independence that one has to admire.

FREUD Independence is hardly an adequate word for her.

ELIZABETH Oh?

FREUD (*He gets her crutches during this*) She's a tyrant.

49

Sometimes I scarcely dare treat a patient without consulting her. But I have to make some concession. After all, we can't afford to pay her what she's worth.

ELIZABETH I didn't mean Kathy.

FREUD Oh? Madame Freud?

ELIZABETH Yes.

FREUD Yes. Interesting, that you call her "independent."

ELIZABETH If a woman has the man she needs and loves, nothing can touch her or harm her.
(He holds out the crutches but she doesn't take them)

FREUD Have you . . . ever been in love?

ELIZABETH *(Ignoring his question)* Where did you meet?

FREUD In my own home.

ELIZABETH Oh?

FREUD Very brazen of her, wasn't it?

ELIZABETH Well . . .

FREUD No, the truth is, she came to visit my sister. I had only one glimpse of her . . . and . . . I was lost!

ELIZABETH That's the way love should be. At first sight.

(ELIZABETH *starts to lower her legs, but she is obviously in pain*)

FREUD Are they worse today?

ELIZABETH Oh, no.

FREUD The way you move them—
(*He is bending to examine them. She fends him off*)

ELIZABETH No! Please!
(*He does not insist, draws back. She rises*)

FREUD You haven't answered *my* question.

ELIZABETH I've only been close to one person in my lifetime. Charlotte.

FREUD Your sister.

ELIZABETH And my friend. If you'd known her, charming, sensitive, bright . . . and for all her suffering, kind, and pleasant.

FREUD Since her death you've been alone.

ELIZABETH Even now, in the morning sometimes, before I'm fully awake . . . I'm "aware" of her. I sit up suddenly, look around the room expecting . . . but of course she's not there. Oh, the impression I must be giving you. You must think I'm shut off from the world, a recluse! Do you?

FREUD (*He can't deny it*) No—

A FAR COUNTRY

ELIZABETH Well, I'm not. I go to concerts, the theatre. And we have parties . . . sometimes. Teas, very often. In fact, our house in Doebling is one of the most popular in the entire suburb. It's always so alive, so interesting. Conversation, laughter, musicales, people . . .

FREUD (*Pointedly*) *Young* people?

ELIZABETH Young people. And when the weather is good, we . . . I . . . I serve out in the garden. In the spring with the flowers, people say, "Let's go to von Ritters for tea and roses."

FREUD You said "we" . . .

ELIZABETH It used to be that Charlotte and I would serve . . . She would sit there in this . . . you see, her heart made her an invalid . . . this bower of roses . . . she would sit there and pour, cut the cake and I would carry the . . . (*She breaks off suddenly*) Of course, now I sit there, pour, and others move about and carry and serve. If there's one thing I can't bear, it's women who chatter. You must come visit one day. I know, I'll send the carriage for you. And for Madame Freud, of course. (FREUD *does as is usual now, goes to the door and opens it for her, but she stops him with—*) I mean to tell you . . . every day . . . I do admire these. I have from the first time.
    (*She indicates the collection of statuettes*)

FREUD My one vice . . . my only extravagance. Aside from cigars.

ELIZABETH I thought they were gifts . . . from your wife.

52

FREUD No. That one is . . . (*He goes to the collection on the desk*) Ernutet . . . Egyptian goddess of fertility.

ELIZABETH (*She interrupts him*) This one! It was on your desk the first day, was it not?

FREUD (*Turning back to her*) Yes. A new piece I brought with me from Nancy.
  (FREUD *takes the Janus from the shelf and holds it. Since she has both hands occupied with crutches, he displays it to her carefully*)

ELIZABETH A head of Janus! Or must one say the heads of Janus? (*Admiring it*) Magnificent! Is it Etruscan?

FREUD My collection, like your poetry, may not be quite what it seems. A copy. In fact, most of these are.

ELIZABETH But a very fine copy! (*As she admires it, and they are physically close, she says suddenly*) As long as we are exchanging confidences . . . I've written several poems . . . to you.

FREUD I would like to read them.

ELIZABETH Would you?

FREUD Yes.

ELIZABETH I . . . There are no endings . . . eleven poems . . . and not one ending.

FREUD Some day, when they have endings will you let me read them?

ELIZABETH Someday, perhaps. Though . . . there are some poems no one will ever see. I destroy them . . .

FREUD Why? Are you afraid of something? Are you?

ELIZABETH I can't describe it.

FREUD Try. Please?

ELIZABETH You wouldn't understand. No one could.

FREUD If you tried . . . I might.

ELIZABETH (*Feeling the overt symptoms of an anxiety attack*) I . . . please . . . I . . . it's getting dark in here. I . . . I can't breathe . . . it's a feeling . . . sometimes I feel that I'm falling . . . yes, falling . . .

FREUD No earth beneath you . . . only a void . . . dark . . . empty void . . . (*She looks at him suddenly, pleading yet wondering*) Yes! There are others who feel as you do!

ELIZABETH Then, maybe you can . . . oh, God . . . I can't . . . I can't . . . they hurt so!
          (*She trembles so, her crutches fall away. She is about to collapse but he catches her and assists her to the couch. He kneels quickly, examines her legs. What he sees makes him stand back, shocked*)

54

FREUD Elizabeth, how did you get those bruises?

ELIZABETH Last night . . . I . . . stood in a long dark corridor . . . suddenly at the end of it, a door opened. A bright light. And a man. He beckoned to me. I wouldn't move. Till I saw it was you. I started toward you. As I reached the door, you slammed it in my face. I beat on it. Cried out, "Open! Help me! You promised. I believed you. Now help me!" You didn't . . . open. I woke. In terror. Alone . . . in the dark. "I will do it without him, without crutches," I said. Dragged myself from the bed. Rose to my feet. Even took a step . . . then they crumpled . . . I fell . . . lay there on the floor . . . hating them and I . . . I beat them and beat them and beat them! God, she buried the wrong daughter! (*During the above,* FREUD *has been unable to comfort or reassure her. With her final outburst and tears, he turns, looks to the Faraday machine and decides to at least divert her. He goes to it, and moves the machine toward her. The movement makes her ask*) What is that?

FREUD It may soothe your pain. (*He turns on the machine, holds aside her skirt and runs the glass over her lower legs, creating sparks*) There, now. Well?

ELIZABETH (*Assessing it*) I feel no change.

FREUD (*He turns, adjusts the batteries*) Now?

ELIZABETH No difference.

FREUD (*Applying the rod*) You feel no difference at all?

55

ELIZABETH Can't you make them stronger?

FREUD (*Giving it no special significance, he turns up the current, applies the rod*) Now?

ELIZABETH Wait! Yes! That *is* better!

FREUD (*Puzzled that she can think so*) Better?

ELIZABETH The pain is going away! More, please! Make the sparks stronger! Stronger! (*Puzzled, yet intrigued by the phenomenon. He deliberately adjusts the current and observes that though it obviously hurts, she says*) Much better! Much much better! Oh, yes . . . yes . . .
(*Her exhilaration becomes very great till he suddenly turns off the machine. She looks up at him, puzzled*)

FREUD Elizabeth . . . you're sure it feels better . . . that the pain's not so bad?

ELIZABETH Oh, yes! For the first time in a long time, the pain almost went away.

FREUD And now, when you move them?

ELIZABETH (*She tries to move them and there is obviously some pain there*) Well, naturally, when I move them.

FREUD (*Still unconvinced*) But it did feel better?

ELIZABETH Oh, yes. I like this treatment. I like it very much. Why haven't you tried it on me before?
(*The doorbell rings*)

FREUD   . . . I wanted to observe you thoroughly first.
   (*He goes to pick up her crutches from the floor*)

ELIZABETH   We shall have to use it tomorrow. And every day from now on. Won't we?

FREUD   Elizabeth! I *know* that current of such intensity is very painful. I've tried it myself. Yet you insist you feel better?

ELIZABETH   Infinitely better. It was worth enduring the current. I think you've found exactly the treatment for me, Doctor.

FREUD   As long as you feel better.
   (*He opens the office door and starts leading* ELIZABETH *out.* FREDERICK *enters through the front door*)

ELIZABETH   Oh, I do. I do. I haven't felt this well in months. Months!

FREDERICK   That's wonderful, Lisl! In fact, if you're up to it, why not a ride around the Prater this afternoon?

FREUD   Why not, Lisl? I recommend it!
   (MARTHA *enters the anteroom, carrying a length of fabric and a ball of crochet yarn*)

ELIZABETH   If my doctor says so, of course!

FREDERICK   Splendid! Oh, did Elizabeth tell you? We met Dr. Taussig at a dinner party one evening. He's delighted with the way she's looking.

FREUD Oh? Good. Good
    (*He goes back into the office*)

ELIZABETH Madame.

MARTHA Fräulein. (ELIZABETH *and* MARTHA *exchange nods of greeting as* FREDERICK *leads* ELIZABETH *out.* MARTHA *enters the office, still carrying the fabric and ball of yarn*) Isn't it wonderful?

FREUD Wonderful?

MARTHA (*As she drapes the fabric on the arm of a chair, she does not notice his reaction*) That she's feeling so much better.
    (*She is displaying the fabric and yarn but he doesn't look*)

FREUD She is *not* feeling better.

MARTHA (*Interested in her fabric, she asks casually and rhetorically*) Then why would she say she was?

FREUD Reassurance.

MARTHA If you only reassure her, that's more than the other doctors were able to do.

FREUD *She* was reassuring *me!* That's the kind of medicine your husband practices. The patient has to reassure the doctor because the doctor is sure of nothing. But the

58

strangest thing . . . I haven't done anything for her, yet she's afraid I'll send her away. Why?

MARTHA (*Paying no attention, since she's involved in draping the fabric*) Look, the ruffle for the crib. Instead of heavy velvet or a dark shade, how do you like this? And then a crocheted border of this . . . to give it color. Of course, this is for a boy. If it's a girl, they have exactly the same yarn in a pink . . . (*She is quite sure he is paying no attention at all*) If it's a girl, we might drown her. Like they do newborn kittens. Don't you think? My dear?

FREUD Whatever you say, Princess.

MARTHA Sigmund!

FREUD I'm sorry, Princess. Fakery! Yet she insisted it helped her!
(*A sudden urge of anger and frustration overwhelms him and he lifts the rod and smashes it on the floor*)

MARTHA Sigmund!
(*She starts, like a good housewife, to pick up the pieces after laying aside the fabric and the ball of yarn*)

FREUD (*Tries to stop her*) Princess! Don't! You'll cut yourself!

MARTHA And how would you notice?

FREUD Princess! !

    (KATHY *rushes into the room, having heard the crash of glass*)

KATHY Good heavens, what happened . . . Oh, you dropped it. (*She goes at once to kneel on the floor and pick up the pieces*) Here, let me!

    (KATHY *lays out her dustcloth to serve as a container for the pieces*)

FREUD Be careful. Both of you! . . . (*The doorbell rings to interrupt him*) *I'll* answer.

KATHY Oh, no! How would it look? The doctor answering the door himself.

FREUD Kathy, you finish this.

KATHY It would be a reflection on *me*.

FREUD Kathy, please. Finish this. I'll answer the door!

KATHY But, Herr Doctor, it's not right.

FREUD (*Joking with her*) *I'll* finish this, you answer the door.

KATHY No! In all my years of service, no doctor I worked for ever answered the door himself—

    (*She is interrupted by* BREUER's *entrance. He looks in, cautiously, then explains*)

BREUER Evidently no one heard my ring.

FREUD   My fault. It seems I'm not up on my medical protocol. So we were having a little meeting of the Academy here. (*This last is directed to* KATHY) It's all right if he joins us, isn't it? He's a very fine physician.

KATHY   (*Righteously*)   I have my work to do. Excuse me. (*She gathers up the corners of the cloth and carries off the glass fragments*)

FREUD   (*As soon as* KATHY *is gone*)   At that, she knows more than some doctors I've seen. Well, Joseph, how are you?

BREUER   (*Gives his hat and gloves to* MARTHA)   Better than I should be, worse than I'd like to be.

FREUD   We could all say that.

BREUER   (*To* MARTHA)   And my patient is doing well, I assume.

MARTHA   (*Smiling*)   Some coffee? A little streusel? (*She takes* BREUER's *coat*)

BREUER   Ah, that—Yes. How could I refuse? A man could keep up the appearance of prosperity simply by having coffee and streusel at the Freuds' once a week. Always so much butter in your cake. Mind you, Martha, do not cut down. Only you must not tell me. (MARTHA *exits*) Frankly, Sigmund, rather than coffee . . .

FREUD   A schnapps.

BREUER Please.

FREUD (*As he gets schnapps and glasses*) Joseph, I'm glad you're here! I was going to come see you. Your case! I read it! It's the most startling case I've ever read! But it's incomplete! All the notes aren't here.

BREUER Sigmund! Did you talk to Stegel?

FREUD Yes. Where is the rest of it?

BREUER What did you tell him?

FREUD Who?

BREUER Stegel! What did you say to him?

FREUD He treated Fräulein von Ritter at one time. I wanted to find out what he used. Now, where's the rest of your—

BREUER (*Interrupting*) Did he mention hypnosis, or did you?

FREUD *I* did, I suppose.

BREUER Well, damn it, Sigmund, it's all over Vienna today! Three times I heard it mentioned in the General Hospital!

FREUD Well?

BREUER Well? Hypnosis is a foul word in a doctor's vocabulary, yet you go about using it freely, recklessly!
    (*He takes the file from the desk*)

FREUD Joseph! You're taking it back?

BREUER Yesterday you talked to Stegel, who happens to be the head of the Ethical Practices Committee, and you mentioned hypnosis. Who knows, tomorrow you may decide to discuss my case with someone.

FREUD But I gave you my word!

BREUER With your enthusiasm? What if you blurt it out? No, it's too dangerous. I cannot take that chance.

FREUD "Blurt it out" . . . "too dangerous" . . . You use that kind of language about a conspiracy. Not about a *medical* case. Doctors have a right to know about this, Joseph. It's startling, unprecedented.

BREUER There! You see? Next, you will convince yourself it's your *duty* to tell them.

FREUD Not mine, yours! You're a doctor of standing. It's your responsibility.

BREUER Sigmund, what happened to this girl is misleading— You said yourself the file is not complete, so you have no right to draw any conclusions.

FREUD Complete or not, one thing is obvious. Symptoms that doctors like me are defeated by every day, you cured!

BREUER There! You see what I mean! You were always the first to condemn it. Now you're doing it yourself!

63

FREUD Doing what?

BREUER The word "cured," *you're* using it now!

FREUD And why not? (*He opens the file. He finds the page*)
Listen! Your own words . . . "Thus from that time on, the
patient overcame her inability to swallow fluids." I call
that cure! And this . . . ". . . once the cause was revealed,
her coughing spells disappeared." Cure!!

BREUER My instinct was right. I never should have let you
see this. It is not a case history! It's a diary, containing
events, not evaluations. And not *all* the events at that!

FREUD Then *tell* me all the events!

BREUER You will forget the whole matter!

FREUD You can't tempt me with this and then expect me to
forget it!

BREUER It's very easy to exaggerate what happened!

FREUD She had many symptoms. They were cured. Is that
an exaggeration?

BREUER It's an exaggeration to think that this can be of any
help in any other case!

FREUD Why do you say that?

BREUER Because I know what's going through your mind.

64

Your patient, Elizabeth, and this girl, you've been making comparisons between the two cases.

FREUD Yes. They are the same in a number of striking ways! Your patient, from your description, a young woman of high intelligence, very attractive, but unmarried.

BREUER Because she had to nurse her sick father.

FREUD My patient's situation exactly!

BREUER If you really insist on making comparisons, my patient hypnotized *herself*. Does yours?

FREUD No, nor can I hypnotize her.

BREUER Then these cases are *not* the same, are they?

FREUD Granted . . . still . . .

BREUER Sigmund, this whole process is not as simple as it would appear, or as safe. I cannot tell you the torture this girl went through.

FREUD Tell me, Joseph! True, it may well lead to nothing. If you don't tell me it will surely lead to nothing. Joseph?

BREUER (*Finally*) Do you promise not to jump to outrageous and unjustified conclusions?

FREUD Promise.

BREUER What do you want to know?

FREUD Start with the first time you found her in that state of self-hypnosis, the words she spoke . . .

BREUER I stopped by on my usual evening visit. I went into her room. She happened to be asleep, so I started to back out when suddenly I heard her say "torment . . . torment . . ." Thinking she spoke to me, I asked, "What torments you, why?" But her answer was totally unrelated to my question.

FREUD Except, of course, that all this . . . is about things that *did* torment her. Memories that tormented her. That's what excited me so! Because, Joseph, that fits exactly with Charcot's theory! He used to say to me, "These patients, they suffer from their memories." Your patient purged herself of her tormenting memories and she was cured of the symptoms!

BREUER There, you see! An unjustified conclusion! She was never cured of her paralysis in the legs.

FREUD (*Momentarily defeated*) You're right. And yet it seems . . .

BREUER (*Interrupting*) Nothing in this case was ever what it "seemed" to be. Nothing! Ordinarily under hypnosis you ask a patient a question, she answers. This one didn't. She *avoided* answering. Finally, I even gave up asking questions. I simply let her talk and she did; on and on and on. And when at last a memory *did* come out, there was no

BREUER She was so terrified. She gasped, and that sound woke her father. "What is it?" he demanded. And all she could think to say was . . . "Nothing, Father . . ."

FREUD (*Supplying it*) . . . "Nothing, Father. I just coughed. That's all. Go back to sleep."

BREUER Exactly.

FREUD And from that time on just hearing music always gave her terrible coughing spells. A fantastic kind of logic! But even more fantastic, she merely related the incident to you and was cured of her symptom. Cured!

BREUER Sigmund—you're using that word again!

FREUD Yes!

BREUER (*Pointedly*) And I *remind* you again, her *paralysis* never was *cured!*

FREUD Why did you just say that?

BREUER Because you cannot make a theory out of one case. If I learned anything it was that this procedure had to be *voluntary,* just as her self-hypnosis was voluntary. If I asked her questions she would never answer. But in a few days, in her own time, in her own way, she would arrive at the same subject. She could not be forced. It could only come out of her a little at a time . . . (*He sees the ball of yarn* MARTHA *has left on the chair*) . . . as . . . as one unwinds yarn from a ball. Remember that, before you go forcing a treatment on . . .

FREUD   Repeat that!

BREUER   She could not be forced—

FREUD   No, no, no. "Unwind yarn from a ball . . ."

BREUER   Yes?

FREUD   Where does that come from? Somewhere . . . someone unwound yarn from a ball . . . The legend! Theseus! . . . unwound yarn from a ball and left a trail so he could find his way back through a labyrinth. The cave of the Minotaur, the labyrinth!

BREUER   Sigmund, let's not confuse mythology with medicine.

FREUD   What you said, that *isn't* mythology! You said your patient had to unwind her thoughts slowly, like yarn from a ball, in order to find her way back to her memories. Joseph! Maybe there's a labyrinth in the mind . . . that hides secret memories, and uses them to torture us.

BREUER   Sigmund!

FREUD   The kind of memories Charcot used to talk about. Don't you see, it fits!

BREUER   Sigmund!!
        (*They are interrupted when the door opens and* MARTHA

enters, carrying a tray with a coffee pot, cake plate, cups and saucers. FREUD *goes to her, at the same time exploding)*

FREUD It fits! He found it! He found it!

BREUER Sigmund, *I* make no claims for this case.

FREUD (*Ignoring* BREUER's *protest, he is too engrossed in telling* MARTHA; *turning suddenly on* BREUER) How long ago was this?

BREUER Six years.

FREUD Six years??? (*To* MARTHA) Six . . . did you hear? (*To* BREUER) Charcot was alive then! If only he'd known!

BREUER Sigmund, wait . . .

FREUD (*Afire, he can't be stopped*) He searched all his life and never found it. *You* found it and never told anyone! Maybe the unseen wound is memory! Guilty memory!

BREUER You must not consider this a . . .

FREUD (*Overriding him*) Maybe that's what leaves people crippled, stuttering, blind . . .

BREUER Sigmund, you're drawing unfounded conclusions again!

FREUD Unfounded? Why? Look what you've done! You've

held the autopsy *before* the patient died. Found the wound. Cured it! I can use the word now! Cured!

BREUER Remember . . . this is not complete!!

FREUD Complete or not, there's enough in there to convince anyone! And you kept it secret. Joseph, caution may have made you a successful doctor. Now be a great one!

BREUER Sigmund, you will listen to me! Before you attempt something that may have fatal consequences!
(MARTHA *reacts, causing* FREUD *to say*)

FREUD He doesn't mean that.

BREUER Don't I? There are things not in here . . . important things. Probably the most important. I would rather not have to tell you this . . . even now . . .

MARTHA (*Misinterpreting his reluctance*) I could leave . . .

BREUER You had better stay! (*Both* FREUD *and* MARTHA *react, puzzled*) You are involved in this, too.

FREUD Joseph?

BREUER Yes. First, it is unusual for a doctor to see one patient as frequently, or for such long visits as came to be the habit in this case. But she seemed to welcome my visits. And for myself it was the most exciting and interesting case I've ever had. It was like looking through a microscope into a living human brain at work. I talked of little else at home.

Till an unfortunate thing began to happen. My patient was getting better, but my *wife* was becoming unhappy, morose. She had grown jealous of the patient who was, after all, an attractive girl. Once I was aware of that I decided the treatment had to stop at once. Since my patient was feeling much better, although she was not completely cured, I went to call on her one afternoon and told her that it was finished.

FREUD   What did she say?

BREUER   Not much actually. So I went away feeling greatly relieved. Till that night. I was summoned to her house by her mother. I arrived. I found her worse than she had ever been. All her symptoms had returned . . .

FREUD   *All* of them?

BREUER   And a new one . . . Pseudocyesis . . .

FREUD   A false pregnancy?

BREUER   So advanced she was already in the throes of delivering. Rhythmic pains, distension, she was going through it all. And speaking to *me* as the father of her child.

FREUD   She was that much in love with you?

BREUER   So much, that her life was in my hands. And I didn't want it!

FREUD   What did you do?

73

BREUER I . . . I hypnotized her . . .

FREUD You were able to do that?

BREUER And told her that when she awoke she would feel better, calmer, and all her symptoms would be gone.

FREUD And were they? Joseph—

BREUER I . . . I don't know . . .

FREUD But, you . . .

BREUER The . . . the next morning . . .

FREUD (*Forcing it out of him*) The next morning!

BREUER I left the city. I took my wife to Venice. On a second honeymoon.

FREUD Joseph, you . . .
        (*He does not say it*)

BREUER Go on . . . "You deserted a patient in serious trouble. A patient who might have destroyed herself." Say it! You should! It was entirely possible she would commit suicide. And I knew it! But I was so frightened by what I'd done that I turned from a patient and ran.

FREUD Joseph, the patient . . . what did become of her? Do you know?

BREUER She's in an institution.

MARTHA God.

BREUER The strange thing . . . during the day I understand she is quite well. But at night . . . at night the symptoms all come back. And there are delusions. At night she is quite mad. Let that be a warning to you. (*He consults his watch*) I didn't realize. But I'm already late for an important consultation. (*He takes the file and starts out, but stops at the door. To* MARTHA) I didn't want to involve you. I did only because in the end, you may suffer most.
(*He exits*)

MARTHA Why was he warning you? Sigmund?

FREUD That girl had a relapse and he was frightened. I can understand that. But when you look beyond the danger . . .

MARTHA She lives out her life in a sanitarium!

FREUD Yet underneath it all, there is one fact! For a time, granted for a brief time, he did cure her! That means something!

MARTHA And that the patient is destroyed?

FREUD What do you think is happening to Elizabeth? She is slowly destroying herself. We're willing to accept that. We stand by and watch it happen. Why not risk, explore, and perhaps discover!

MARTHA But, Sigmund, to risk driving a sick girl mad? (*He doesn't answer. She knows the futility of talking to him when he's this way. She pours the coffee, watching him all the while. He picks up the yarn, weighs it. She holds out coffee to him. He is unaware of it*) Sigmund . . . ?

> (*He is too involved. She sets down the cup, stares at him an instant, and then exits. The sound of the door closing makes him briefly aware of her*)

FREUD Princess . . .

> (*He is unaware that she is gone. He turns to take the coffee cup, but suddenly tosses the ball to the floor, holding one end of the yarn and letting it unwind. Then he begins to reel it in slowly*)

The Curtain Falls

Scene 2

Time: afternoon, some days later.

At rise: we find AMALIE FREUD *sitting in her son's office, attired in street clothes and hat. She holds herself like a classical statue of a suffering mother, grieving and deeply pained, yet trying to seem brave.* DOLFI, *who is with her, tries to penetrate the pose and persuade her to leave.*

DOLFI Mama, what if a patient arrives? It could be embarrassing.

AMALIE Hasn't it dawned on you yet? Half an hour we've been here and no sign of a patient.

DOLFI His consultation hours don't start for another ten minutes.

AMALIE And who says people only become ill to fit the doctor's schedule? Not a single knock on the door. Not a single emergency.
(KATHY *enters*)

DOLFI Martha—

KATHY Madame isn't back yet.

AMALIE It's stuffy in here. Open the window.

DOLFI Mama . . .

AMALIE Open the window!
(DOLFI *goes to do it*)

MARTHA (*As she enters by the front door*) Kathy.

KATHY Madame.
(*She uses this to warn* MARTHA *of trouble in the office*)

MARTHA (*Realizing now, she hands over her packages and bags to* KATHY) Thank you, Kathy. (MARTHA, *unpinning her hat and taking it off as she crosses, turns back at the door to find* KATHY *holding the bundles and gawking*) Kathy . . . into the kitchen.
(KATHY *exits.* MARTHA *enters the office*)

AMALIE Child, when she told me I didn't believe it. But when *he* repeated it I had no choice!

MARTHA Mama, what's wrong?

DOLFI Dr. Schoenfeld again!

AMALIE This is not a matter for children!

DOLFI God may work in mysterious ways. But not Mama!

AMALIE Dolfi!!

MARTHA What did Dr. Schoenfeld say?

AMALIE   As far as any of them can remember, this has never happened before!

MARTHA   What?

AMALIE   The appointments at the hospital . . . this time not a single Jewish student! And he said it was Sigmund's fault.

MARTHA   How could it be?

AMALIE   Reprisals!

MARTHA   For what?

AMALIE   A patient almost every good doctor in Vienna has failed with . . . and Sigmund thinks he can cure her. Of course they resent it!

MARTHA   Mama, don't try to frighten me! Will they do anything to him?

AMALIE   I don't mean to frighten you. But it is terribly dangerous.

DOLFI   You exaggerate!

AMALIE   Do I? He gave us his word! He said, "I'm finished with such patients. There's nothing I can do for them." Did he say that? (*To* MARTHA) Did he?

MARTHA   He has a right to change his mind!

AMALIE (*She goes to* MARTHA) Defend him. Loyalty is your finest trait. But defend him when he's wrong? You want to, I know. I did the same with Jacob. If he was in trouble I hid my fears from him. But I was wrong! I should have asked more, thought more of myself!

MARTHA Mama, I don't care for myself.

AMALIE Of course not.

DOLFI Martha, don't let her! Mama, how can you even . . .

AMALIE Dolfi! Be still. Not another word!

MARTHA Even Breuer says it is dangerous.

AMALIE And Breuer is his friend. Think what the others must be saying.

MARTHA Joseph even said that . . .
   (*She stops abruptly*)

AMALIE Said what? Child?

MARTHA Mama, I . . . (*She turns away.* AMALIE *goes to her*) I can't talk to him. I'm afraid to intrude on his work. And sometimes I even feel that we don't exist for him at all, the baby or I.

DOLFI Martha, no!

MARTHA I feel that way. I do! Frightened. Alone. Shut off.

And I don't know how to tell him. Mama, is it natural for a woman to feel afraid all the time, now? Is it?

AMALIE (*Takes her in her arms*) No, child. But I understand. And if it becomes too difficult for you, stay with me till the baby comes.

DOLFI Mama!

AMALIE Dolfi!

DOLFI Because Papa disappointed you, you don't trust Sigmund to make his own life. It's not fair. Leave them alone!

AMALIE Will you stop!

DOLFI Leave them alone!
(AMALIE *slaps* DOLFI *across the cheek, silencing her*)

AMALIE The young who have not even lived know so much more than we who have seen and suffered . . . and have such bitter memories! Yes! The night we had to abandon our home in Freiburg. *I* was a wife. *And* a mother. With Sigmund by the hand, you here. And yet not more than a child myself. We stood on the railroad platform late at night. Misty, cold. Papa carrying two small valises, everything we owned in the world. And he kept staring down the track, searching for the train. But only to avoid facing me. Because his little weaving mill failed, we had to give up our home. Had to go to a strange and hostile city. I couldn't help being terrified. Even the poverty I knew in Freiburg seemed better than the uncertainty of Vienna. But

81

I told myself, you must not cry. He feels bad enough. Then the sound of the train whistle cut through the night and I . . . when I heard the whistle . . . saw the light of the train . . . felt its grinding roar rushing at me, I wanted to hurl myself under it! I will save them from the fear and the disappointments! I tightened my hold on Sigmund so he could not get away from me. And I moved forward till I felt his little hand suddenly grow ice cold in mine . . . as though he sensed . . . and then I . . . I couldn't do it . . . couldn't. (*To* DOLFI) But for that, you might have died before you were even born. Maybe greatness is too much to ask. But before I die, I have a right to see him established, safe, secure. A right to know that my daughter-in-law, my grandchild, won't go through anything like that.
(*The doorbell sounds*)

MARTHA   Sigmund . . .
(*The door opens abruptly and* BREUER *enters*)

BREUER   Sigmund! Sigmund!!
(MARTHA *opens the office door*)

MARTHA   Joseph!

BREUER (*Entering the office*)   Oh, Martha, I beg your pardon. (*To* AMALIE *and* DOLFI)—Madame, Fräulein—Where is Sigmund?

MARTHA   He should be here now. What is it?

BREUER   I have something I want to show you. (*Takes a letter out of his inner pocket*) I expected this to happen, but not so soon. Listen to this! From Stegel! *(He finds the place in the letter)* ". . . your colleague's treatment of this girl might be deemed highly unethical when judged by the majority of the doctors in the Academy . . ." He tampers with a case of Stegel's and now Stegel is poking his sharp thumb into my guts and saying, "Jew, keep your Jews in line else there'll be trouble."

(FREUD *opens the front door and enters to catch the last few words*)

AMALIE Exactly what Schoenfeld said! *(To* DOLFI) So I needn't defend myself!

FREUD *(Enters the office, saying lightly—)* If someone defends, someone else accuses.

(The solemnity is brought home to him as BREUER *hands him the letter. He reads it)*

BREUER I don't want any of us to face charges of unethical conduct!

FREUD Joseph, I would discuss it with you now but I'm expecting a patient . . .

BREUER *(Interrupting)* You know what they're saying now. "That Jew Freud is using witchcraft to cure a girl the great Stegel couldn't help."

FREUD "Witchcraft" . . . from you, Joseph?

BREUER It's their word!

AMALIE And you'd better listen, Sigmund!

FREUD Mama, your trouble is you were born with all the pretensions of a Hapsburg and all the restrictions of a Jew.

AMALIE (*Interrupting*) What will happen if Gentile doctors are already using the word "witchcraft"?

FREUD Prove to me that any doctor failing to say what he thinks can help put an end to prejudice and I will consider *saying* nothing and *doing* nothing.

AMALIE Sigmund, the world is theirs! We only live in it!

FREUD Wouldn't it be better if we explored the human mind to find out why men hate, rather than take on the color of the walls hoping they won't hate us because they can't see us?

AMALIE So now it's a doctor's responsibility to cure hatred. God hasn't been able to do that! There is no changing you, is there, my son? . . . (*She turns from him to* MARTHA) My home is always open to you. Dolfi.
    (*She exits.* DOLFI *follows*)

FREUD Princess? Princess, what did she mean, her home is always open?

MARTHA They always say to a pregnant woman, now you must eat for two. Well, now I must be afraid for two.
    (MARTHA *exits and when* FREUD *would follow her,* BREUER *arrests him*)

BREUER Sigmund, you will settle nothing out there. Her trouble, yours, mine must be settled in here. Sigmund, if they call hypnosis "witchcraft" what will they say about further experiments? "The soul of a man is a far country which cannot be approached or explored." That statement is as true today as it was in Heraclitus' time. You cannot tamper with the human soul! It's like a blind man doing surgery.

FREUD There is no other way for her.

BREUER She won't be the first patient for whom there was no other way at all! What is this obsession you have about her?

FREUD Your patient was cured. Granted, only for a time, but cured.

BREUER Her paralysis was *never* cured. Why? Ask yourself that! As I have! Because her memories must have been so bad that she chose to cling to the paralysis rather than face them. A patient is better off paralyzed than insane. I can tell you that!

FREUD Next you'll say she's better off sick than well!

BREUER You've never seen a patient almost destroyed by fear, self-reproach, mental torture of the worst kind. Else you wouldn't be so brave, so reckless. And don't tell me once again, my patient was cured. Because there is a differ-ence . . . Yes. With my patient I had an anaesthetic. I could hypnotize her. What you propose is like operating

85

without an anaesthetic. What will happen when your patient is face to face with what she wants to hide . . . when her sanity hangs in the balance? What can you do then? Sew up the wound? Say the operation is over? Oh, no. This is a terrible kind of surgery. With no instruments, no anaesthetic, no knowledge, no experience.

FREUD First-year medical school . . . The patient who complains of pain all over has pain nowhere.

BREUER I will not discuss your patient's symptoms!

FREUD And *your* symptoms!

BREUER What are you talking about?

FREUD Some patients complain of pain all over. You have *reasons* all over. Don't do it. It will destroy the patient. Don't do it. It will destroy the doctor! It will hurt the Jews! It's like a blind man doing surgery! Always "Don't do it." But the reasons keep changing. Why? Because none of those is the real reason. Joseph, why are you so afraid?

BREUER Because I no longer have the extravagant courage of youth! Damn it, look at me. The epitome of the successful Viennese doctor! Well, I wasn't always. I started as a poor Jew too. Took my share of injustices. Bit my tongue and watched other men passed over me at the hospital. And I promised myself they won't defeat me. Not Breuer. I have brains, skill, training. And one more thing. Attractiveness. I am the kind of doctor women will consult more for what I am than for what I know. That's not a very pleasant thing to face, for a serious doctor. But a Jew must enter through any door he can. So I swallowed my pride, worked hard at this bitter little game, and now I want the respect, the security, the comfort. I *like* to be welcomed in the best homes in Vienna. I worked for it. Bit my tongue long enough. Earned it. From now on all I want is for my world to hold together for the rest of my life. But you come along and say, let's startle them! Let's tell them! Let's blow up the world! Not my world, you won't. Oh, no!

FREUD Aha! Now I know. That's it! I should have realized it the first time you told me about her. You think there will be a scandal. Don't you? Well, this time *you* exaggerate.

BREUER Do I?

FREUD What if it did come out that this girl fell in love with you? Where's the crime? Why must that be wrong? Every doctor knows the patient who recovers best is the patient who trusts him. We call it having confidence in the doctor. And we are not ashamed of it.

BREUER That's quite different from being in love with the doctor!

FREUD Precisely! (BREUER *reacts*) Yes, I think that the reason that girl *was* so spectacularly helped was that she *did* trust you, that she *was* in love with you. Because as long as she was, she grew better symptom by symptom. That must have some meaning.

BREUER Sigmund . . . listen to me . . .

FREUD Love may be an element in a cure. Love may have therapeutic value. There may be great significance in the patient's falling in love with the doctor. Why not let that come out finally?

BREUER And what . . . if it came out that Breuer fell in love with the *patient?*

FREUD Joseph!

BREUER See what it does! Even to you. Yes, *that* was the crime. To encourage her love and then become frightened by it and run away. Even now I ask myself: How did this happen to me? Was it because she needed me? Made me feel there was some magic in me that could help her? Or was it for less noble reasons? The usual sordid situation of a middle-aged man flattered by the love of a pretty young girl? I always wondered, the first person I would tell this to, what would he say. Now I know.

FREUD I was only thinking, he can't allow a personal fear to stand in the way of such an enormous discovery.

BREUER I'm sorry, Sigmund.

FREUD Joseph, if it is like doing surgery in the dark, I need you, your knowledge, your support!

BREUER I will not endanger my security!

FREUD Civilizations rise and fall. We have museums full of proof! And men pretend there is security! It's a trap. A disease.

88

BREUER An incurable disease, unfortunately. And a trap. Once you have it, you discover how many necessities of the spirit you can no longer afford. Freedom to hold an opinion. The right to take a risk. Precisely the reputation you think makes me strong is what makes me vulnerable. (*He starts out, stops just long enough to say—*) The fault is yours. You asked courage of a man who had only caution to give.
> (*The doorbell rings.* FREUD *crosses to open it. He does, and finds* ELIZABETH, *on crutches as usual, but holding an object in a felt bag.* FREUD *invites her in*)

FREUD Good day—

ELIZABETH Doctor—

BREUER Fräulein—

FREUD ELIZABETH—
> (*He indicates the office. As she enters,* FREUD *and* BREUER *exchange looks.* BREUER *exits.* FREUD *follows* ELIZABETH *into the office*)

ELIZABETH Such a lovely afternoon.

FREUD Elizabeth—I wonder if . . . (*She is seated now and holds something out to him—a wrapped object*) What is that?

ELIZABETH Open it and see.

FREUD (*He unwraps it*) Another Janus?

ELIZABETH *The* Janus. The *original*. Do you like it? Will you add it to your collection?

FREUD You must have searched every antique shop in Vienna!

ELIZABETH It wasn't *in* Vienna. They found it finally in London.

FREUD You went to all that trouble?

ELIZABETH It was the only way. I alerted every dealer on the Karntnerstrasse. Then every other day I made the rounds myself. Till finally, yesterday, there it was. You will keep it, won't you?

FREUD Elizabeth . . .

ELIZABETH (*Quickly*) The other day you called me Lisl . . .

FREUD Lisl . . . it is a very touching thing, very thoughtful . . . *this.* (*He indicates the Janus*) But at the moment, very embarrassing. It's been a rather . . . difficult . . . day for me. Would you mind if I asked you to come back to-morrow?

ELIZABETH Of course, if you don't feel well . . . or are too tired . . . or if you don't *want* to see me . . .

FREUD If it hadn't been such a difficult day . . .

ELIZABETH We patients forget that doctors have troubles . . .

but that's because we're so taken up with ourselves. Of
course, I will excuse you . . .

FREUD Thank you.
  (*She starts to put her crutches in place to get up. But
  though she strains, she cannot move. She trembles with
  tension and fear*)

ELIZABETH Doctor, I can't move them.

FREUD Try!

ELIZABETH I can't.

FREUD You can't move them at all? (*He puts aside the Janus
  and kneels at her side to press her legs, test them*) Can you
  feel that?

ELIZABETH Yes.

FREUD Yet you say you can't move them?

ELIZABETH I can't. Can't. (*Shakes her head*) Now it *will* be
  the wheel chair!

FREUD (*He rises, moves back from her*) Lisl . . . do you
  trust me? I must know!

ELIZABETH (*Looks up, puzzled*) Trust you?

FREUD If you do, I may be able to help you.

ELIZABETH How?

FREUD I can't explain. I can't promise it will work or even
that it will be safe. But if you ever want to walk, this is
the only hope I can offer you.

ELIZABETH Hope?

FREUD A new treatment.

ELIZABETH Will it hurt?

FREUD Not in the way you think of pain now.

ELIZABETH *(She considers, then—)* I trust you. Whatever
you do.

FREUD This is something that *you* do.

ELIZABETH I? What?

FREUD You must . . . remember. And talk.

ELIZABETH Remember? Talk? About what?

FREUD Memories . . . deep inside you.

ELIZABETH What kind of memories?

FREUD Memories. Some of them distasteful . . . painful . . .

ELIZABETH Distasteful memories . . . about what?

FREUD I don't know, so I can't tell you. But you know.

ELIZABETH I don't know anything. There's nothing to remember.

FREUD Do you believe that I'm trying to help you? Do you believe that? (*She nods*) Then do what I ask of you. Lie back . . . think . . . let your thoughts unwind slowly . . . like yarn from a ball.

ELIZABETH Unwind?

FREUD Yes. (ELIZABETH, *puzzled, tries, then suddenly turns her head away*) Elizabeth? (*She looks to him, startled, confused*) Just then . . . when you moved . . . what did you remember?

ELIZABETH I didn't remember anything.

FREUD Then what made you move?

ELIZABETH I *didn't* move.

FREUD (*Her obvious contradiction makes him try*) All right, then, try again. See what you *can* remember.

ELIZABETH About what?

FREUD About anything.

ELIZABETH That's ridiculous.

93

FREUD Why?

ELIZABETH Because you don't want me to remember just anything. That doesn't make sense.
(*She touches her right leg at the thigh*)

FREUD (*Noticing, he asks quickly*) Right now. What did you remember?

ELIZABETH Nothing.

FREUD Nothing about pain in the legs?

ELIZABETH No.
(*But she does remove her hand hastily*)

FREUD.. (*Trying to stimulate thinking and talking*) Elizabeth . . . that first day . . . when Frederick brought you here . . . I asked how long you'd had the pain and you said . . .

ELIZABETH (*Usurping his thought*) I explained that! He was talking about slight pain. But I said, "The first serious pain was two years ago." That's exactly what I said. And it's true. Did you think I lied to you?

FREUD No, it's just an interesting inconsistency . . .

ELIZABETH I explained it once. There's no need to do so again!

FREUD Then tell me, was there any connection between the slight pain and the serious pain?

ELIZABETH Slight pains turn into serious pains. That's only natural.

FREUD Isn't it more natural for pain to grow less, to disappear eventually.

ELIZABETH Mine didn't!

FREUD Exactly. Why?

ELIZABETH I know why you're doing this! To revenge yourself on me.

FREUD Revenge?

ELIZABETH Yes. Because you couldn't hypnotize me. Because your electric current failed. I didn't blame you. I even brought you a gift. Why do you want to make my pains worse?

FREUD (*Using the admission*) *Are* they worse now? Why? Did you remember something? What?

ELIZABETH I remembered nothing!
(*She turns away from him. He rises, moves behind her, flexes his fingers, then applies them in a slight rotating motion to her temples, at the same time turning her back so he can look down into her face*)

ELIZABETH Why are you doing that?

FREUD To help you concentrate . . . to help your thoughts to unwind . . .

ELIZABETH They don't want to unwind! And even when they do . . . they don't make any sense!

FREUD (*To draw her out*) Don't they?

ELIZABETH No. In fact, I . . . I . . . well, it has nothing to do with what you want to know!

FREUD Perhaps not. Tell me anyhow. What did you just remember?

ELIZABETH It really doesn't matter! (*He doesn't answer. She is silent a moment, then—*) That . . . that day . . . those men carrying my father into the house. The day he had his first heart seizure. I was holding the door open for them. I looked down at his face. So pale, lying limply to one side . . . like the head of a broken doll I had once . . .

FREUD (*Thinking he's uncovered an important fact*) You saw him that way and then you felt the pain in your leg!

ELIZABETH No.

FREUD You're sure?

ELIZABETH I'm sure!

FREUD (*Failing, he tries a new tack*) Then can you remember anything that *does* have to do with pain in the legs?

ELIZABETH You seem to think there's something to remember. Maybe you know. What do you want to find out? Ask me! If I know, I'll tell you. I have no secrets. Nothing to be ashamed of!

(*But her pain is worse and he notices*)

FREUD What were you thinking of . . . just then?

ELIZABETH Thinking . . . nothing! Well . . . nothing connected with what we were talking about . . . At night . . . at night he would call for his medicine. "Lisl." When he called that way you didn't keep him waiting. I would get up, not even stop to put on my slippers, and run barefoot across the floor to his bed. The floor . . . icy cold . . . I used to hate . . . used to hate to touch that floor. Oh.

FREUD Yes?

ELIZABETH That was the first pain . . .

FREUD So the first pain had to do with your father.

ELIZABETH No. With the floor! I used to hate that . . . that floor!

FREUD And *that* was the first pain. (*She nods*) And in your right leg?

ELIZABETH Yes, it was right here, in the right leg. Oh, I can move it again.

FREUD Go on.

ELIZABETH What?

FREUD You were talking about your father. Go on.

ELIZABETH I loved him so. To see him . . . sick all the time . . . to know that he was going to die . . .

FREUD And during all that time you took care of him?

ELIZABETH Nursed him . . . bathed him . . . fed him . . .

FREUD During that time, did you ever ask yourself, why is it my duty to care for him? Why not my mother?

ELIZABETH Oh, she couldn't do it.

FREUD Why, was she ill?

ELIZABETH No. She couldn't do it as well as I. Sickness always made her very uncomfortable, even then. He liked my taking care of him. He always said, "Lisl, you have the touch of angels in your fingers."

FREUD And you?

ELIZABETH I?

FREUD Did *you* like it?

ELIZABETH Of course. He was my father.

FREUD So you never resented it.

ELIZABETH I loved doing it. Just as he loved to have me do it.

98

Every morning I would bandage his legs. Set his leg down on mine. Right here. Gently. First one . . . round and round . . . tight. But not too tight. Support, the doctor said, but don't cut off the circulation. Then pin. And set down. Gently. Never hurt him. Never. And he would smile at me. Then the other leg . . . set down . . . round and round . . . tight but not . . .
> (*Panic makes her grip her right thigh at the exact place*)

FREUD (*Picking up and finishing for her*) Not too tight. Day after day after day. (*She nods*) Lisl, in all that time, did you ever say to yourself, I would rather not do it?

ELIZABETH A man with a bad heart, you *have* to bandage his legs.

FREUD But you don't have to *like* it.

ELIZABETH I did like it!

FREUD Did you?

ELIZABETH Yes!

FREUD A girl as lovely as you, as vivacious, never said to herself, I'm young I want to live *my* life. Not *his!*

ELIZABETH Never.

FREUD I want to be courted, taken to dances, to parties. Never said that?

99

ELIZABETH No!

FREUD Never said, I don't want to spend my life chained to his bedside?

ELIZABETH No!

FREUD I want to be free.

ELIZABETH No!

FREUD Never once felt, I won't be free till my father is dead! I wish he were dead!

ELIZABETH (*Stunned by this sudden truth, she is silent, then reacts in horror*) Dead? Oh! No! Oh! No!!

The Curtain Falls

ACT THREE

Time: morning, some weeks later. The faint light of the early day seeps into the office where the lowered blind is not flush with the window frame. There is enough light to reveal the figure of FREUD *slumped in impromptu sleep over his desk, which is spread with opened books and pamphlets used in a night of hectic research.*

MARTHA *enters from the upstage door. She is beginning to show her advancing pregnancy. She comes down into the anteroom and raises the shade of the small window to light up the room. Then she goes to the front door and unlocks it in accord with the morning routine. She is now interrupted by* KATHY *entering from kitchen carrying a breakfast tray with a large steaming coffee pot.*

KATHY *comes across to the office door, but* MARTHA *intercepts her and examines the tray to make sure it is properly arranged.*

KATHY Madame—

MARTHA He will want more butter with his rolls. (*She lifts the lid of the coffee pot, sniffs*) Good. (*She dips a finger into the cream pot and tastes, evaluates*) Still sweet. You may take it in, Kathy.

KATHY Madame, for a quarrel to go on so many weeks . . .

MARTHA Kathy!

KATHY Yes, Madame . . . Shall I *say* anything?
(KATHY *has been trying to be a peacemaker during the weeks—but* MARTHA *discourages her*)

MARTHA Only, "Good morning, Herr Doctor." Understand?

KATHY (*Let down*) Yes, Madame. (*She goes to the door, supports the tray against the frame, knocks lightly, then opens the door and enters. She comes in, sets down the tray on the table, goes to the window and raises the blind, flooding the room with light and waking* FREUD) Good morning, Herr Doctor . . .

FREUD Oh . . . Good morning, Kathy. (*He rubs his eyes, stretches as he rises. He sniffs and becomes aware of the coffee*) Already?

KATHY Yes, Herr Doctor.
(*She picks up the tray and comes to the desk.* FREUD *has been rooting around in the ash tray for a cigar butt, finds one, clamps it in his mouth and sees the look of distaste on her face*)

FREUD You're right! (*He tosses the butt back into the ashes*) An evil smell. Evil. (*He turns to the breakfast tray to use that action to cover his real intention*) More butter, please, Kathy? And how is Madame this morning?

KATHY The same.

FREUD No change in the prognosis?

KATHY I'm not supposed to say, sir.

FREUD That bad?

KATHY (*Almost tearful*) Yes, sir.

FREUD (*He dips a finger into the cream, tastes*) Still sweet.

KATHY (*Tearfully*) How long is it going to go on this way, sir?

FREUD Now, Kathy . . . (*He shrugs, hopelessly*) The gift of speech is wasted on women . . . Whenever they have something really important to say, they cry instead.

KATHY I'm sorry, Herr Doctor.

FREUD Now, you take this out . . . (*Indicating the full ash tray*) . . . while I change.
(*He exits.* KATHY *starts straightening up. In the anteroom,* MARTHA *is lingering, doing unnecessary straightening up, so she can ignore him when he comes out. She does. He stops to say—*)
Good morning, Princess.

MARTHA (*Proper, cool*) Good morning, Sigmund.

FREUD I . . . I had to work all night again. Not that it did any good. In all the medical literature I can't find anything that will help me with Elizabeth's case. Weeks and weeks without any way to reach her. I can't break through.
(MARTHA *does not answer. Suddenly—*) Princess, I . . .

*(He stops when she turns to look at him forbiddingly.
Then he makes a small "sorry" gesture and exits through
the upstage door.* MARTHA *goes into the office, looks
around, is distressed by the disorder and the smell, and
starts to help* KATHY *as well as to give orders)*

MARTHA Kathy, take that ash tray out at once!
(She goes to throw open the window)

KATHY Yes, Madame.
(She exits, taking the ash tray with her. MARTHA *closes
up books and pamphlets, unable, however, to do so without looking at them to see what he's been reading. While
. . doing so, there is a sharp sound at the front door.
. . . sest to the door, exchanges a look with* MARTHA
. . . early intrusion.* MARTHA *signals.* KATHY *opens
the . . or.* FREDERICK *enters, carrying* ELIZABETH *in his
arms)*

MARTHA Good God! What happened?

FREDERICK This is your husband's fault!

MARTHA Why? What did he do?

FREDERICK Where is he?

MARTHA What happened?

FREDERICK *(He has carried* ELIZABETH *into the office and set
her down on the couch)* There! Now, Elizabeth, I insist

you tell him. Don't be afraid. (ELIZABETH, *pale and seemingly exhausted, only nods*) Where is he?

MARTHA   He'll be out in a moment.

FREDERICK   I will wait for him.
(FREDERICK *nods and, closing the door, exits into the ante-room, leaving* MARTHA *and* ELIZABETH)

MARTHA   What did he do?

ELIZABETH   (*Ignoring her question*)   How old are you?

MARTHA   Twenty-seven . . . why?

ELIZABETH   Why did you wait so long to have a child?

MARTHA   A young doctor . . . waits to establish a practice . . . waits to get married . . . waits to have children . . . a young doctor waits for almost everything.

ELIZABETH   And the young doctor's wife waits with him . . .

MARTHA   She has no choice, once she chooses a doctor.

ELIZABETH   Yet it is not such a sacrifice as it seems! Is it?

MARTHA   (*Reacting to hostility*)   Perhaps not . . .

ELIZABETH   All the time she knows. She knows—that one day it *will* happen. A woman can wait a long time if she knows that.

MARTHA Yes.

ELIZABETH What does it feel like once you know? Do you just accept it or are you aware of it every moment from that time on?

MARTHA (*Softening*) You accept it. And you're aware of it.

ELIZABETH Do you think very often about what the pain will be like when it actually happens?

MARTHA *I* used to worry about that too. But I will tell you . . . (ELIZABETH *turns away suddenly*) He's trying to help you. He's doing all he can.
　　(*But* ELIZABETH *cannot be consoled.* MARTHA *exits to fetch* FREUD, *who enters now.* FREDERICK *intercepts him*)

FREDERICK Dr. Freud!

FREUD What happened to her?

FREDERICK Did you order her to go to the cemetery and stand at the family graves?

FREUD Then she went!

FREDERICK What did you possibly hope to achieve by that?

FREUD I won't discuss that with you now.

FREDERICK You *never* seem to have time to discuss Elizabeth with me. You tell her to go to the cemetery as if it were

part of some medieval ritual, and she goes. Well, Herr
Doctor, she collapsed. And now she can't use her legs at all.

FREUD Did she feel any pain?

FREDERICK You *wanted* her to feel pain, didn't you?

FREUD Yes. Because pain is the only language she knows.
Through it she revealed her feelings to me. Without it I am
completely cut off from her. The cemetery was a desperate
effort. If it failed, I'm sorry. Now, get out and let me go to
work!

FREDERICK Doctor, I warn you . . .

FREUD Herr Wohlmuth, you don't realize how dangerous
this can be now! Please, go!
(*He turns to the office door*)

FREDERICK Even Taussig, who recommended you, said we
are justified in going to the Medical Academy about you!
(FREUD *turns back*) Yes! Her mother and I, we talked to
Taussig. He thinks you're mad!

FREUD You'd better go!

FREDERICK I promised her she could see you today, but I'll
be waiting outside that door.
(FREDERICK *stares at* FREUD *defiantly, then turns and exits.*
FREUD *goes into the office to greet* ELIZABETH)

FREUD Good morning, Lisl . . . how do you feel today?
(*There is no answer from her*) . . . No crutches today?

ELIZABETH Frederick carried me in.

FREUD Did he carry you into the cemetery too? (*She looks at him sharply*) Did he?

ELIZABETH No.

FREUD But he did carry you out. What happened? Did you feel any pain?

ELIZABETH I feel no pain. I feel nothing. I can't use them at all. I disappoint you, don't I? You wanted me to suffer.

FREUD To react, yes.

ELIZABETH But I did react.

FREUD Oh?

ELIZABETH Yes, we have . . . *I* have decided . . . that I will not come here again.

FREUD I see. Well, you're a patient, not a prisoner. You're free to go, if you choose. Only, before you do, I would like to say it's interesting that you didn't cry, didn't feel any pain at the cemetery!

ELIZABETH You're accusing me of something.

FREUD I only said it was interesting.

ELIZABETH It was the way you said it! Lately you've done nothing but accuse me.

FREUD If you talked *I* wouldn't have to. And then I wouldn't "accuse." Did you think about what I asked you yesterday?

ELIZABETH You asked me a great many things yesterday!

FREUD About the pain.

ELIZABETH I've already told you everything I know about pain!

FREUD You've never told me why lying down is worse than sitting—or standing.

ELIZABETH I never said it was!

FREUD (*Behind her*) Elizabeth, think, remember. The first time that happened.

ELIZABETH It never happened! Besides, what good does it do to keep remembering all the terrible things over and over again?

FREUD (*Trying a new tack*) Elizabeth, the day they brought your father home ill, you stood at the door, looked down, saw him, and felt a pain in your right leg.

ELIZABETH I told you that!

FREUD Yes. But can you remember another time when you were also *standing, looking down* and you felt pain?

ELIZABETH I . . . Oh . . .

FREUD Yes?

ELIZABETH You mean at Charlotte's bedside . . .

FREUD Was it at Charlotte's bedside?

ELIZABETH When I reached her bedside and she was dead, I felt a pain . . .

FREUD In the *left* leg?

ELIZABETH Yes, it was in the left leg . . .

FREUD Lisl . . . think . . . try to think why sometimes you feel pain in one leg, sometimes in the other?

ELIZABETH I don't want to talk about pain any more!

FREUD What would you *like* to talk about?

ELIZABETH Since this is the last day, I would like to talk about you.

FREUD Oh?

ELIZABETH But you'll be angry with me.

FREUD No, say anything you feel like saying. I won't be angry.

ELIZABETH How do I know?

FREUD I give you my word.

ELIZABETH If I could see your face, I'd know.

FREUD If you wish. (*He comes around from behind the couch*) Now, what did you want to say?

ELIZABETH (*After a brief pause*) Something has happened to you. You've changed.

FREUD Have I?

ELIZABETH Yes. In the beginning I believed you wanted to help me. That you were my friend. That's why I told you all these things, things I would never reveal to anyone else. But it seems that isn't enough. You always want to know more and more and more. And you want to know only the painful things. I've come to think that your only purpose is to hurt me, that's why I won't come here again.

FREUD And why would I want to hurt you?

ELIZABETH I don't know. You want me to remember more and suffer more. Is that what a doctor is supposed to do? Make people suffer?

FREUD A doctor is supposed to cure people. And sometimes pain is part of the process. Elizabeth, bring yourself to really talk about the pain again.

ELIZABETH No! . . .
    (*She sets herself aggressively, looking away from him*)

113

FREUD Elizabeth? Elizabeth. Elizabeth . . .
   (*He moves with each word till he is back behind the
   couch*)

ELIZABETH (*Suddenly*) You are a Jew!

FREUD (*Surprised; hurt but controlled*) Yes.

ELIZABETH (*Regretful, she seeks to re-establish contact*) If
   you would touch your fingers to my temples again, then I
   could talk . . .

FREUD If it would help . . .
   (*He starts to place his fingers on her temples*)

ELIZABETH I need to see your face!

FREUD All right. (*He moves around to sit on the edge of the
   couch, places his fingers at her temples*) Now, Elizabeth,
   if you will talk . . .

ELIZABETH (*Correcting him*) Please, call me Lisl . . .

FREUD Lisl . . . if you can talk about why the pain is worse
   sometimes in one leg, and sometimes in the other. Concentrate on that.

ELIZABETH (*She suddenly reaches up and puts her arms around
   him and draws him to her*) If only you loved me! Then
   I would get well! (FREUD *frees himself firmly yet gently
   and draws away from her*) I embarrassed you. Now you *do*
   hate me. Don't you? (FREUD *doesn't answer but keeps*

114

watching) Say something! (*He still doesn't answer*) Please, say something.
(*She twists around to try to see him*)

FREUD Don't turn around.

ELIZABETH I need to see you!

FREUD Don't try. Just keep talking! Talk!

ELIZABETH I can't.

FREUD Then we'll wait till you can.

ELIZABETH I'll . . . I'll talk if you touch my temples.

FREUD (*His first instinct is to accede to her request, but then he stops himself and moves back*) Now, Elizabeth . . .

ELIZABETH Lisl . . .

FREUD Elizabeth, you will talk . . . without any fingers at your temples. Without any contact at all. We will go back and talk about pain, standing, walking, lying down. Pain . . . in all its forms . . . as *you* know it.

ELIZABETH If you would only touch . . .

FREUD (*Interrupting*) Talk.

ELIZABETH About what?

FREUD About pain. Now begin.

(FREDERICK *enters alone. He goes carefully to the office door to hear what is going on inside*)

ELIZABETH Where?

FREUD Anywhere. Just begin.

ELIZABETH I don't know where . . .

FREUD What about the first time you felt the pain while lying down?

ELIZABETH I don't remember anything like that!
(*Now* MARTHA *comes out to find* FREDERICK. *Whatever were her feelings before, she has been touched by* ELIZABETH. *She addresses him crisply and with disapproval*)

MARTHA Herr Wohlmuth! (*Surprised at his eavesdropping, he swings around aggressively*) What are you doing there?

FREDERICK (*Aggressively and self-righteously*) She should have told him. She should be out here by now. Why isn't she?

FREUD You don't?

ELIZABETH No, I don't. Besides I'm tired. Too much has happened to me today . . .

MARTHA Come away from that door!

FREDERICK I have a right to know what is happening.

(ELIZABETH *becomes aware of* FREDERICK'S *voice from outside. It*

MARTHA (*Interrupting with the kind of fierce protection of a mother for her young*) Get away from that door!

FREDERICK She's my responsibility. Remember I brought her here. Placed her in your husband's care. Now I insist that she leave.

MARTHA (*Interrupting firmly*) *You* will leave. Or you will wait out here. Or you will come inside and have coffee. But you will not go in there. (*Relaxing just a little*) Myself, I recommend the coffee. Please.

makes her become still suddenly, and tense)

FREUD Elizabeth . . . (*He becomes aware that she listens intently and and is now physically tense, so he does not pursue her with questions. Inside the office,* FREUD *and* ELIZABETH *maintain an air of almost rigid silence as they await the outcome of the struggle between* MARTHA *and* FREDERICK)

(*The silence from outside the door tells* FREUD *and* ELIZABETH *that the difficulty has subsided*)

FREUD Elizabeth! Right now . . . do you have a pain?

ELIZABETH (*Concealing her pain*) No. (*She interrupts him by raising herself. But it is painful*)

FREUD Lie down! (*She sits there, stubbornly refusing to move*) Elizabeth?

117

ELIZABETH I won't!

FREUD Because finally the pain *is* back! And it *is* worse lying down than sitting up! Elizabeth? In which leg *is* the pain?

ELIZABETH The left. Please, I want to go!

FREUD Tell me! All these days when you've said you felt no pain. Were you concealing something from me?

ELIZABETH No.

FREUD Days without pain. Now suddenly the pain returns! And in the left leg! Why, Elizabeth? What happened? What changed?

ELIZABETH Nothing changed!

FREUD We're going to find out. So no matter how much it hurts, lie down! Elizabeth! Elizabeth, tell me about your sister's death. You were at Badgastein with your mother.

ELIZABETH I couldn't help it. I had to go there!

FREUD I know, you were sick! Go on!

ELIZABETH I took the baths . . . I drank the waters . . .

FREUD And?

ELIZABETH My mother said we would stay on till I got well . . . unless . . . Charlotte grew worse . . .

118

FREUD Then you got word?

ELIZABETH Word came in the afternoon. She was worse, much worse. The next train from Badgastein was in the evening. Ill as I was, I insisted we take it. I needed to see Charlotte alive again if it was humanly possible!

FREUD Your mother, what did she say?

ELIZABETH That we need not go unless I wanted it.

FREUD Was that all she said?

ELIZABETH She said she was afraid we would not get there in time.

FREUD What did you say?

ELIZABETH Nothing.

FREUD You didn't try to assure her that you would.

ELIZABETH Oh, I did that.

FREUD That wasn't exactly nothing, was it?

ELIZABETH It was. Because . . . I knew, even then, we never would get there in time.

FREUD *How?*

ELIZABETH I knew, that's all!

FREUD Knew . . . or hoped?

ELIZABETH (*Trying to turn and face him*) There! You see, you're accusing me again.

FREUD (*Ignoring her statement*) What happened?

ELIZABETH (*Finally*) Evening came. We boarded the train. Because I was ill, I had the lower berth. My mother was above me. The train was slower than usual. It stopped and started and crawled along from station to station. Mother kept looking at her watch, opening it, snapping it shut. I couldn't sleep at all.

FREUD The sound of it kept you from sleeping?

ELIZABETH Yes.

FREUD How often did she do it?

ELIZABETH I don't know. Why?

FREUD Every three minutes, five, fifteen?

ELIZABETH Every fifteen or twenty minutes, I think.

FREUD That's not very often. Certainly not often enough to keep you from falling asleep.

ELIZABETH But it did!

FREUD The sound . . . or the *pain?*

ELIZABETH By that time I was used to pain. It was the sound!!

FREUD The grinding of the wheels, the shrill whistle, neither of those kept you awake? Only your mother's watch. *Was it the sound?* Or did you have more pain than usual, that night?

ELIZABETH Oh . . .

FREUD So it was the pain?

ELIZABETH It was the pain.

FREUD Severe pain, while lying down. Was that the first time? (*She nods*) And in the left leg? It was the left leg. (*She nods*) Did you sleep at all? (*She shakes her head*) When you arrived in Vienna the next afternoon you must have been exhausted. (*She nods*) Did anyone meet you at the station?

ELIZABETH My uncle.

FREUD What did he say?

ELIZABETH My mother started to cry, he took her in his arms and said, "Now, now, Bertha." Then he led us to a carriage out of the station.

FREUD And during the ride to the hospital?

ELIZABETH The usual things . . . the doctors were doing all they could . . .

FREUD (*Surprised*) Then as far as you knew she was still alive?

ELIZABETH Yes.

FREUD And when you reached the hospital?

ELIZABETH It was almost evening. We didn't go in the front way. I remember that. She was in a little side building, beyond the garden. I remember as we passed through the garden thinking, "Evening brings the sweetest smells." We went up the path to the open door.

FREUD Who?

ELIZABETH My mother, my uncle, myself.

FREUD In that order?

ELIZABETH No, they let me go first.

FREUD So you were first inside the door?

ELIZABETH (*Nods*) And first to see.

FREUD What?

ELIZABETH That she was covered . . .

FREUD And therefore dead? (*She nods yes*) And then?

ELIZABETH (*Resisting*) I told you this part once before.

122

FREUD (*Persisting*) And then?

ELIZABETH I stood there . . . and suddenly I felt a sharp stabbing pain.

FREUD Very sharp?

ELIZABETH Very.

FREUD Which leg?

ELIZABETH Both.

FREUD (*Pointedly*) *Both?*

ELIZABETH No, it was . . . the left leg.

FREUD And?

ELIZABETH We went to her bedside. Mother lifted the cover. We saw her face. We never saw her again. Never spoke to her. Never did anything for her, but bury her in the ground without even saying good-bye.

FREUD And that's all you remember?

ELIZABETH That's all.

FREUD Have you left anything out?

ELIZABETH No.

FREUD Elizabeth, your sister had been dead how long? . . .

ELIZABETH Not quite an hour, we found out later.

FREUD Yet you say you haven't left out *anything*?

ELIZABETH I haven't!

FREUD When you entered the garden, when you entered her room, was there anyone else there? A doctor, perhaps.

ELIZABETH She was dead! Of what use was a doctor to her then?

FREUD So there was no one there, you're sure?

ELIZABETH No one!

FREUD Not even your brother-in-law?

ELIZABETH No!

FREUD If she just died, he should have been there.

ELIZABETH He wasn't. I know he wasn't! Because I remember thinking as we went through the garden, "Why isn't Frederick here to meet me?" (*He starts*) No, no, that's not what I said. I said, "Why isn't Frederick here to meet us?"

FREUD And then you went into the room and saw your sister covered.

ELIZABETH I told you that part.

FREUD Yes, and your mother uncovered her. You saw her face and your pain became suddenly very sharp in the left leg.

ELIZABETH Yes. And I'd rather not continue.

FREUD You're free to go whenever you wish.

ELIZABETH Thank you.
(*She starts to get up and finds great difficulty because of the pain, but she tries very hard to conceal it*)

FREUD The pain is worse now isn't it?
(*She turns sharply to face him*)

ELIZABETH (*Defensively*) It was that argument between your wife and Frederick. It upset me!

FREUD Yet it's exactly the same kind of pain you felt at the time of your sister's death, when there wasn't any argument.

ELIZABETH That was different! That was because of Charlotte! Because she was dead.

FREUD The man who was out there a moment ago should have been at your sister's bedside.

ELIZABETH I don't know what you mean.

FREUD You yourself asked, "Why isn't he here to meet me?"

ELIZABETH (*Correcting him*) *US!*

FREUD Us! All right, us. Didn't you say that?

ELIZABETH Yes, I said it!

FREUD What else did you say?

ELIZABETH Nothing!

FREUD You stood beside her bed and what did you say?

ELIZABETH Nothing!!

FREUD No thought . . . no words . . . nothing?

ELIZABETH Nothing. Just tears. I began to cry and it seems as if I've been crying ever since. And that's what all the doctors said! Except you!

FREUD What did they all say?

ELIZABETH That it is my grief that makes me this way.

FREUD Your mother loved your sister, and grieved for her, she's not like this. Frederick loved her, grieved for her, he walks on two straight legs. Only you, Elizabeth. Why?

ELIZABETH I told you!

FREUD Grief grows less as time goes by. Yours gets worse. Pain, hobbling, crutches, worse and worse and worse. Why?

ELIZABETH I don't know.

FREUD What of the pain that started before your sister's death, *before* the grief.

ELIZABETH That was different. That was rheumatic pain!

FREUD So the doctors said.

ELIZABETH It was! From walks in the damp evening air.

FREUD Walks not taken alone.

ELIZABETH I told you there were other young people.

FREUD Simply "other young people"?

ELIZABETH What are you trying to say?

FREUD Elizabeth, what are you trying not to say?

ELIZABETH I've told you everything.

FREUD There is still one thing missing . . . the thought . . . the words that went through your mind at your sister's bedside.

ELIZABETH I told you . . .

FREUD Tell me again.

ELIZABETH Please, I'm tired . . . I can't remember any more . . . I don't know what you want me to say any more . . .

FREUD Start with the moment you entered the garden. (*She doesn't pick it up*) You entered . . . realized that Frederick was not there to meet you. Then?

ELIZABETH We . . . went into the room. We saw her.

FREUD Covered?

ELIZABETH Covered. And we went close to the bed and mother uncovered—OH!!

FREUD Elizabeth! Elizabeth . . . you drew close to her bed and what did you think?

ELIZABETH Nothing . . .
(*Unknown to herself, she struggles, rises from the couch*)

FREUD You stood there . . . at the moment of the pain . . . or even *before* the pain . . . what did you say?

ELIZABETH Nothing! (*She is on her feet and moving toward the door with great effort and very slowly*) Nothing!

FREUD Nothing! And yet now you would walk to escape from it? Run, if you could? (*Not moving to help her yet*) Escape from what? Right now! What??

ELIZABETH (*She stands there, trembling and tottering. Suddenly in fear she calls out*) Oh, God. Help me! Help me!

FREUD (*He doesn't move to her*) Elizabeth! What did you think, what did you say, once you *knew* she was dead?

ELIZABETH (*It bursts forth from her*) "She's dead. I'm glad. Now he is free and I can become his wife!" There! I said it! Now you know!
(*She starts to weep and at the same time* FREUD *moves to catch her in his arms*)

FREUD And then the pain? (*She nods without revealing her face. He helps her to a chair, moves behind her to continue*) The pain in the same leg that began to hurt when you just heard his voice out there. The same leg that began to hurt after those long walks you and he took together. Not just "young people"—you and Frederick!

ELIZABETH Nothing happened on those walks.

FREUD No. But one doesn't have any way of controlling one's thoughts, does one?

ELIZABETH Once, during a walk with him, I said to myself, "*I* could give him more love, more understanding . . ."

FREUD More than who?

ELIZABETH More than . . . more than Charlotte.

FREUD And on the train . . . were you going to see her . . . or him?

ELIZABETH Don't, please . . .

FREUD *Say* it!

ELIZABETH Him. But then he wasn't there to . . .
(*She stops*)

FREUD "To meet me . . . ?"

ELIZABETH To meet me . . .

FREUD But once you knew for sure that she was dead, then
your feeling burst forth inside you, "She's dead, he's free,
she's dead, he's free." And suddenly that other feeling . . .
shame for thinking that . . . then pain. That's the way it
was, wasn't it, Elizabeth?

ELIZABETH Don't send me away! Please don't send me away!

FREUD Is that what you're afraid of? If people knew what
went through your mind they'd despise you? So you wrap
yourself in illness, in paralysis, to earn their sympathy instead of their scorn. So they will say, "*Poor* Elizabeth," instead of, "*Terrible* Elizabeth, to desire her sister's husband."
Well, I won't send you away. You'll go when you choose.
And when you go, it'll be by yourself, on your own two
feet.

ELIZABETH (*Unbelieving, she turns to him*) You think it
will be possible for me to walk again without the crutches?

FREUD You didn't need them a moment ago.

ELIZABETH You mean I can . . . *now?*

FREUD It won't be easy. Or without pain. (*She looks at him.*

130

Then he urges her to try. She rises on her own. It takes great effort. Then she takes a few steps, is breathing hard, but she turns to him and smiles) If you want to walk out there to him . . . you can do that, too.

ELIZABETH *(Suddenly fearful)* To him?

FREUD You think I blame you?

ELIZABETH Don't you?

FREUD We will find out if a girl who has suddenly lost her father and is exhausted from months of nursing him is so terribly bad because she falls in love with a young man like Frederick. And if you will permit me, may I be counsel for the defense.
   (FREUD indicates she is free to go. He goes to the door to open it for her)

ELIZABETH I've never opened that door myself. I want to. *(FREUD stands back and she goes slowly toward the door. She hesitates when she reaches it, then smiles at him and opens the door and moves into the doorway. Startled at not finding FREDERICK there)* Frederick! Frederick! Where is . . . *(She is half-turning back to FREUD when FREDERICK, followed by MARTHA and then KATHY, enters from the upstage door. FREDERICK, interrupted in the midst of his coffee, still carries his napkin)* Frederick!
   (She manages a few steps. FREUD follows her into the anteroom)

FREDERICK *(Almost terrified)* Elizabeth! Be careful! You'll fall! You'll hurt yourself!

ELIZABETH No. Look. Look at me.
(*She takes a few slow, careful steps*)

FREDERICK Lisl! Lisl, I had forgotten how you looked without them. Herr Doctor, I'm sorry for the things I said. Thank you.
(*He turns to offer his arm to* ELIZABETH. *She looks to* FREUD, *then takes* FREDERICK's *arm. She turns to* FREUD)

ELIZABETH Tomorrow, Doctor?

FREDERICK Tomorrow?

FREUD (*With an understanding smile at* ELIZABETH, *he says to* FREDERICK—) There is still . . . some work for us to do yet.

ELIZABETH Tomorrow.
(FREUD *walks back into his office and while the action continues in the anteroom he goes to stare at the Janus. Meantime,* FREDERICK *has extended his arm,* ELIZABETH *has taken it, and they start out slowly, when* FREDERICK *realizes that he still has the napkin. He turns to give it back to* MARTHA)

FREDERICK Thank you, Madame. (*A little sheepishly*) For the coffee.
(MARTHA *smiles.* FREDERICK *and* ELIZABETH *exit.* KATHY *exits into the apartment.* MARTHA *goes into the office, where she finds* FREUD *staring at the Janus head*)

FREUD Not two faces. Two minds. The clash of minds creates

Salome Jens and Steven Hill, as MARTHA
BERNAYS FREUD and SIGMUND FREUD

the unseen wound. And like surgeons we have to find it, open it, drain it.
(*He suddenly kisses her on the cheek*)

MARTHA What's that for?

FREUD For helping me. And don't deny it. I heard you. (*He smiles, releases her. She kisses him on the cheek*) And that?

MARTHA (*Smiling*) Because now there won't be any standing at railroad stations late at night. No listening to train whistles. (*She thinks it's pleasantly amusing, till he reacts with a puzzled look*) Don't worry about it. Just something your mother told me once.
(*She exits*)

FREUD Railroads, late at night . . . train whistles . . . (*He turns in the direction of the door, calls out to* MARTHA) Exactly what did Mama say? I must know!!
(*He starts off as the lights come down. The waltz fades in and holds. We are back in 1938. The lights come up and the sound of the doorbell is heard. The* NAZI *opens the door and lets* DOUGLAS *in.* MARTHA *comes on from the apartment*)

MARTHA Herr Douglas.

DOUGLAS Madame, the car is here.

MARTHA Sigmund!

FREUD (*Wheeling himself on in his wheel chair*) And not

only walked, but danced! Remember, Princess, we saw her dancing. Then married, though not to him, but married. With children of her own.

DOUGLAS It's time, sir.

FREUD Time . . . yes. Are they out there? Waiting to see the sick old Jew carried out? Hmm? Savages! Well, we shall have to teach them what is in here. (*He holds up the* ELIZA-BETH *file*) The worst tyranny is within. A human being free within himself is free everywhere. They destroy whole peoples? We will save individuals. And in the end we will outnumber them. We'll let them know that!
(*He puts the blanket aside*)

MARTHA Sigmund, the doctor said . . .

FREUD Are you going to believe a Viennese doctor? (*He gets to his feet*) Princess! Out of this room, I walk.
(*They start out*)

The Curtain Falls